AND THAT'S HOW
YOU MAKE CHEESE!

AND THAT'S HOW YOU MAKE CHEESE!

Shane Sokol

Writers Club Press
San Jose New York Lincoln Shanghai

And That's How You Make Cheese!

Writers Club Press
an imprint of iUniverse.com, Inc.

For information address:
iUniverse.com, Inc.
5220 S 16th, Ste. 200
Lincoln, NE 68512
www.iuniverse.com

ISBN: 0-595-17709-3

To my beautiful wife, Marie.
Her patience allowed this book to happen.
To her, I owe everything.

Acknowledgments

Thank you to everyone who contributed their ideas and
their recipes.
Your suggestions and corrections to my recipes made this
book a success.
To all of you, I owe thanks.

Contents

Introduction

This book was written for the millions of people who share the same belief that homemade items are much better than store-bought. For those who believe that their family and loved ones should enjoy only the best, freshest foods without additives or preservatives. For those who enjoy not just a cup of coffee; but a freshly ground cup of espresso from their kitchen. Those that love bread enough to spend hours preparing a fresh loaf straight from their oven. Those who appreciate good drink enough to try their hand at making their own perfect batch of beer or family wine. Those of you who appreciate the art of food, are not satisfied with mass produced grocery items and want to spend time preparing only the best for their friends and family.

Throughout history, cheese has been one of the most important and nutritious foods that humans have ever consumed. Cheese making was a family affair where cheeses of all kinds could be purchased from local farmers and made fresh in the kitchen. Recipes were handed down through the generations like heirlooms. Cheese making was not just a convenient way to store the nutrition from surplus milk; it was an art form in itself. Unfortunately, the Industrial

Revolution all but exterminated these traditions as millions moved to cities and the left their cheese recipes behind. It takes just as much time to make three pounds of cheese in a kitchen as it does to make 3,000 pounds in a factory. In an age of efficiency, the factories won by churning out tons of processed cheese.

This book will introduce you to the delicious world of homemade cheeses. With just a small amount of elbow grease and just a few pieces of inexpensive equipment, your whole family will enjoy fresh and aged cheeses made with all the love and care that good food brings. Enjoy!

If you'd like to share your experiences with us, or would like even more recipes, please visit us online. We'd love to hear about your cheese making experiences. We will list any updates to this book there too.

www.FoodHowTo.com

A Short History Of Cheese

Cheese has been a part of the human diet many millennia before we even learned to write. Because of this fact, it is hard to tell when cheese first appeared. At least 8,000 years before the birth of Christ, after the ice sheets parted and the climate grew warmer, when humans began to plant and harvest food, they also domesticated herd animals. The propagation of the sheep and goat herds grew and the amount of milk that was gained outgrew what could be used. Perhaps an ancient shepherd discovered that a bowl of milk left near the fire would curdle into a mass of curds that could be eaten. A popular story is that of a nomad wondering across the desert with his day's milk held in a bottle made from sheep's stomach finding that at the end of the day, his milk turned into a solid mass of curds. Figuring that this soured milk is better than no milk, held his nose and downed the cheese. To his surprise, it was tasty and made a wonderful lunch. It was not long before he told everyone he knew and cheese making was born.

From that time on, cheese has become and indispensable store of energy for the early settlements. It could be carried easily when moving and kept well; in fact it got better with age. Cheese also became an important product that could be traded or sold for goods without having to kill any animal in the herd. Cheese literally began a revolution of its own, helping to feed ever-larger settlements and paving the way for towns and villages to grow. Cheese making was a convenient way to preserve milk that would have spoiled into a nutritious, delicious and digestible product. It was much easier to transport cheese as opposed to milk and cheese could be saved until a right price could be had.

Ancient records mention how cheese and butter were made throughout Egypt from about 4,000 B.C. onward. Cheese is mentioned many times in ancient texts, including the bible where David carried ten cheeses to the army before slaying Goliath. In fact, the stadium of Jerusalem was built in the valley called Tyropaeon, meaning the valley of the cheese makers. The ancient Romans celebrated cheese and cheese making as it was a daily item in the ancient Roman's life. The name Parmesan owes its existence to parmigiano, a word meaning "in the Parma tradition." Roman soldiers carried large wheels of Parmesan as this drier cheese was better suited to travel and would last months without spoiling.

By about the first century A.D., cheese makers had widespread knowledge of the process of cheese fermentation and storage. The Romans discovered a critical step in making cheese by adding rennet, which speeds the coagulation of the milk. By adding rennet, the Romans developed the technique for pressing curds that could be turned into hard-cheese. Many of the modern cheeses go back into the history books many centuries. The Monastery of Conques in France mentions Roquefort cheese for the first time in the year 1070. Legend has it that Napoleon named Camembert cheese when he was told it had no name. Cheddar has been around since the mid 1500s, named after the town that created it in England, along with other famous names such as Cheshire and Stilton.

Cheese making in North America was kept on the farms and in homes until Jesse Williams built the first cheese factory in the United States in Rome, New York in 1851. Williams and others after him perfected their commercial cheese making and turned thousand of gallons of milk into thousands of pounds of cheese every day. The art of making cheese at home seemed to be lost forever. Now that our society is grasping to bring back vestiges of the simpler times, cheese making is a craft that is slowly returning to the family kitchen. More of us are trying to relearn the art of self-sufficiency by baking our own breads, brewing our own beer and wine and serving cheeses to our family that were made with all the love and care they deserve. This book will teach you how to bring those traditions back to your home to enjoy.

Ingredients

MILK

Milk, especially fresh milk is the foundation for any great cheese. Cheese has been made from every kind of milk you can imagine. Reindeer, caribou, yak, buffalo, and even the llama have provided milk to feed people for centuries. This book will deal with cow and goat milk, the two most common types used in cheese making today.

There are several components that make up milk. Most of the milk, of course, is water. The rest is made up of proteins, fat, lactose (milk sugar), vitamins and minerals. When we make cheese, we cause the protein in the milk to curdle (solidify) and separate from the water. Cutting, cooking, draining and pressing the curds releases even more water from the curds to produce a solid cheese that can be sliced.

Most of us get our milk from the local grocery store where it has been pasteurized and homogenized. Pasteurization is the process of heating the milk to a temperature high enough to destroy all pathogens. Homogenization is the process of breaking up the fat globules naturally in the milk into very small particles that won't separate out and float to the top. Homogenized milk produces curds that are less firm as those made from whole unprocessed milk, but the difference is barely noticeable.

If you are lucky enough to obtain whole unprocessed milk from a local farm, you will need to pasteurize the milk yourself. Pour your milk into a stainless steel or enamel-lined pot and place that pot into another larger pot containing hot water. Heat the milk slowly to 145° F. Hold the temperature there for 30 minutes. This must be done to ensure that all pathogens in your whole milk are destroyed. When 30 minutes have passed, remove the milk from the stove and immerse in the sink filled with cold water and ice. Stir the milk frequently so that the temperature drops rapidly down to 40-45° F. You can now store your pasteurized milk in the refrigerator until needed.

STARTER CULTURES

A starter culture is a growth of a specific type of bacteria in milk. Bacteria cultures act as a catalyst in the acidification process of curdling the milk. These cultures assure that the proper amount of acid-producing bacteria is present in the milk you will be turning into cheese. These bacteria consume lactose (milk sugar) and give off lactic acid as a by-product. It is the lactic acid that curdles the milk when using bacteria in making cheese.

Most supply stores will sell "Direct-Set" powdered starter cultures. These "Direct-Set" cultures already contain rennet, one of the ingredients that helps to coagulate and solidify the milk. I prefer not to use these as you lose control of how much rennet you add and at what time. If you do decide to use these "Direct-Set" cultures, skip the rennet-adding step in the recipe you are following.

There are two basic types of bacterial starter cultures that are used and are named depending on the amount of heat they require to start the curdling process. Mesophilic bacteria cultures work their best when milk and curds are not warmed higher than 103° F. Mesophilic starter cultures are used to make many popular cheeses such as Cheddar, Feta and Gouda. Thermophilic starter cultures can tolerate higher temperatures, to 132° F. are used in making hard Italian and Swiss cheeses.

You can purchase starter cultures in a powder form and keep in the freezer for months. These powders contain the bacterial culture and are very convenient to use. Because they are commercially prepared, you will get consistent results every time. These starter cultures eliminate the need to prepare and cook your own starter culture. However, you can easily make your own starter cultures that can be kept in the refrigerator for a few days or in the freezer for several weeks. A whole chapter in this book is dedicated to producing your own starter culture.

Although any mesophilic starter culture that you buy from a cheese supply store will work for a cheese that requires it, some stores sell variations. For instance, you can purchase MA Mesophilic Culture (lactococcus lactis ssp cremoris) and MM Mesophilic Culture (lactococcus lactis). While both cultures are well suited for making a Gouda cheese, the MA Mesophilic Culture imparts a creamier, almost buttery flavor into your cheese that help bring out the flavor of a good Gouda. Don't hesitate to ask your supplier for advice and recommendations. All suppliers listed in the back of this book are knowledgeable and friendly.

RENNET

After the starter culture has been added to your milk, you will also add rennet in many cases. Rennet contains a natural enzyme, rennin that ripens the milk and causes it to form a solid curd.

Rennet is available in a liquid and tablet form. Both forms have been standardized and are easy to use. Today, rennet is made from animal or vegetable derivatives. The vegetable rennet is produced from the mold Mucor miehei and is available in both liquid or tablet form. The tablet form is easier to store since it does not need to be refrigerated like the liquid form, but is not as easy to measure exactly.

SALT

Many recipes call for salt as it is important in bringing out the flavor and texture in your cheese. It is recommended that you purchase a flake salt, much like salt for pickling, for use in your cheese. Most kosher and sea salts work well and are inexpensive. A good salt will make a noticeable difference in the taste of your finished cheese. In most recipes, salt is added to the curds just before they are pressed. Avoid using iodized table salt as the iodine can affect the cheese making process.

Supplies And Equipment

Most of the equipment that you will need to make cheese can be found right in your kitchen. If you like spending time in the kitchen, you are sure to find most of the tools needed for making cheese hidden in a drawer. Although you may need to purchase a few items, most are inexpensive and can be purchased from local stores or from the suppliers listed in the back of this book. *All equipment* that will come in contact with the milk will need to be cleaned and sterilized before each use. Improper sanitation is the leading cause of failure when making cheese.

These are the items that you may need for your recipe:

POTS. For most recipes, you will need two pots, one large enough to fit the smaller one inside, like a double boiler. The larger pot will contain water that will be directly heated on the stove that, in turn, heats the milk in the smaller pot. Make sure to have a small rack of some sort that will fit into the larger pot for the smaller pot to rest on. This will allow the hot water to completely circulate around the smaller pot. Use only glass, stainless steel or enamel-lined pots. Other metals such as aluminum give off unpleasant flavors to the milk and can actually hamper the cheese making process.

DAIRY THERMOMETER. Your thermometer should read up to at least 212° F. You may use either a floating glass thermometer or a dial thermometer. The dial thermometers are faster and usually have brackets that will hold them to the side of the pot. The thermometer used in this book, and pictured on the previous page, is a digital thermometer. It allows for quick reading of exact temperatures.

MEASURING CUPS AND SPOONS. Use only glass or stainless steel.

CURD KNIFE. Your knife should be stainless steel and be able to reach the bottom of your pot without the handle touching the milk.

STIRRING SPOON. Use only a large stainless steel stirring spoon or ladle.

CHEESECLOTH. Make sure you use only high quality cheesecloth from a supplier. It is much thicker and lasts much longer than the cheap version sold in grocery and hardware stores. Good quality cheesecloth can be used over and over. Simply wash *after* each use and boil in water to sterilize *before* each use.

CHEESE MOLDS. These are used to give shape to your cheese and hold the curds together when pressing. Molds come in all sorts of sizes and are made from a food-grade plastic or stainless steel. You can even make your own molds using yogurt and cottage cheese containers. Simply punch holes from the inside in a regular pattern to allow the whey to drain.

CHEESE PRESS. These are needed when making any hard cheese. They apply pressure to the curds to form them into the mold and squeeze out whey. You can purchase a Wheeler press from a supplier for many years of trouble-free use. Applying pressure by hand, the Wheeler press has a gauge that shows the current pressure in pounds. Many other less expensive presses are available at supply shops and stores listed at the back of this book. In this book, I use a simple plastic mold that cost only a few dollars. It came with a small plastic follower that fits snugly on top of the cheese and presses evenly on the curds when a weight is applied. Even a homemade press can be built using many things you'll find at home. Weights are placed on top to apply the needed pressure to the curds. You can use anything heavy, including a gallon jug of water. (A gallon of water weighs approximately 6 pounds.) For greater pressure, many people stack barbell weights on top of the mold. Make sure that you have a follower made of either wood or plastic that will fit into the mold snugly. You will place the weight on top of this follower. If it does not fit snugly, curds will seep out of the sides, ruining your chances for a great cheese.

If you would like to make your own cheese press, surf over to our website at *www.FoodHowTo.com* for instructions and diagrams!

CHEESE MATS AND BOARDS are used to rest and drain your cheese. The mats, made from bamboo or plastic allow the cheese to air-dry after it has been pressed and the boards are used when draining your cheese. Small towels can be used instead of mats if they are clean and have been sterilized.

SPRAY BOTTLES will be needed if you plan on making mold-ripened cheeses.

SANITATION

Making a good cheese requires absolutely pristine working conditions. Any unfavorable bacteria that come in contact with any of your equipment poses the risk of contaminating your whole batch of cheese. There is no getting around this rule: *Sanitation Is The Key To Success.*

Be sure to sterilize your countertops and any equipment that may come in contact with your cheese with hot water. Boiling your utensils in a pot of water will do the trick; just make sure they are cool before handling. The most convenient way is to run all of your equipment and utensils through your dishwasher without any soap. If your dishwasher has a drying feature, turn it on as this heats the air to a temperature that will sterilize everything. If you do not have a dishwasher available, you may create a bleach solution using 1-2 table-spoons of household bleach per gallon of water. Soaking your equipment in this solution will also kill any bacteria. Make sure that your equipment is rinsed well after using bleach. Any bleach residue left can ruin your plans for a tasty cheese.

The Art Of Making Cheese

Whether you decide to make a quick and easy cream cheese or take the time to age a sharp blue cheese, you will find that the cheese from your kitchen tastes much better than the commercial versions found in your local grocery store. Your cheese will not contain additives, artificial preservatives, artificial colorings or gums. While a cheddar or blue cheese requires a few rounds of practice, most cheeses simply require fresh milk, bacteria, enzymes, a little work and a small amount of time.

Whether you are making cheese from cow's, sheep's or goat's milk, every cheese starts with just a few basic ingredients, much like making bread, beer or wine. But the combination of these few ingredients, time and temperature provide for a wide variety of tastes and styles. There are several steps that you will proceed through when making any of the cheeses in this book. Some require just three or four, while some cheeses require many more steps. The soft, fresh cheeses will only require a few steps since they will not be pressed or molded. The harder cheeses that require pressing and aging will require most of the steps listed in this chapter.

Follow your recipes carefully. All of the steps that you may encounter are listed in this chapter, in the order that you will usually find them in your recipe. The cheese that you decide to make may contain just a few or most of these steps depending on its complexity.

HEATING THE MILK.

Fresh, pasteurized milk from your local store needs to be heated to a temperature that encourages the growth of bacteria cultures that you add to the milk. To prevent burning, always use a double boiler to heat the milk. If one is not available, a large pan, big enough for your pot to fit in can be used. Fill the pan with one or two inches of water that will indirectly heat the pot of milk. Use a rack to make sure that the pot does not touch the bottom of the pan. Heat the milk very slowly. No more than 2-3° every five minutes until the desired temperature is reached.

COAGULATING THE MILK.

The coagulation of the milk is what produces the solid curd. There are two basic ways to perform this step, using acid coagulation and rennet coagulation and can be used independently or in varying combinations depending on your desired cheese or the recipe you are using. Acid coagulation occurs after the addition of an acidic substance such as vinegar or the addition of a bacteria starter culture, which turns the lactose (milk sugar) into lactic acid. Rennet coagulation occurs with the addition of rennet, an enzyme that reacts with the milk forcing it to curdle. Most rennet available today is produced from a vegetable extract. Years ago, rennet was only available as an extract from the stomach of calves. For certain types of cheeses, coloring or additional flavors are added during this stage as well.

ACID COAGULATION.

Bacteria cultures start the souring (acidification) process and impart a characteristic flavor to your cheese. There are two forms of bacteria cultures that can be used.

A dry, powdered bacteria culture can be added directly to the milk. These powdered cultures are very reliable and easy to use. No preparation is needed and they are added directly to the warmed milk once it has reached the temperature required by the recipe.

There are two types of bacteria cultures, mesophilic and thermophilic. Make sure you use the proper culture for the cheese you are producing and be very careful to control the temperature of the milk. Many batches of cheese have been ruined because the temperature of the milk was too high or too low. If you are using a "Direct-Set" powdered starter culture, do not add more rennet, it is included in the bacteria culture.

A homemade starter culture can be added instead of a powdered bacteria culture. A starter culture is a growth of bacteria culture that can be used to make more and more culture. Making your own starter culture avoids having to purchase more powder as you can make your own. To learn how to produce your own starter cultures, please see the next chapter.

CUTTING AND DRAINING. In this step, the curds are cut, allowing the whey to separate from those curds as they drift to the bottom. The curds are then drained for a few minutes to a few hours. Some soft cheeses get drained and are ready to be eaten right away. Others, such as cheddar, get drained, salted and transferred to a mold for pressing.

COOKING THE CURDS. Stirring the cut curds to loosen them and slowly heating them will separates even more whey and produces a firmer curd. All hard cheeses proceed through this step to make sure that the curds are firm enough to hold their shape when molded. Be careful to heat the cheese very slowly, no more than a few degrees every 5 or 10 minutes. To prevent the curds from sticking together, make sure you follow the recipe's instructions for stirring the curds.

DRAINING THE CURDS. The curds, once cooked are transferred to a colander to drain slightly before being transferred to a mold to be pressed. This step removes most of the whey.

Don't waste the whey! The fresh whey that is draining off of the curds can be used to make ricotta cheese. Ricotta can only be made from very fresh whey no more than about an hour old.

TRANSFERRING THE CURDS.
The curds, once drained, are spooned or ladled into the cheese mold or press where even more whey will be extracted.

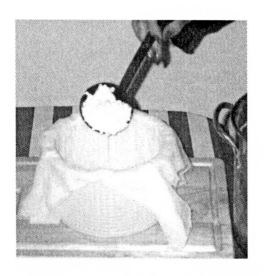

MOLDING AND PRESSING. Once transferred into the mold or press, the cheesecloth is folded over the top of the cheese. A plastic or wood follower is placed on top of the cheese, which just fits into the mold. Weight is added on top of the follower. This shapes the cheese and rids the cheese of even more whey. Several harder cheeses require pressing for days where the cheese is flipped frequently to prevent any dry spots. Any type of weight can be used. Even dumbbell weights can be stacked on top of the follower. Here, we have used a jug of water to press the curds. A gallon of water weighs approximately 6 pounds. To make your own mold and press, surf on over to our website *www.FoodHowTo.com* for instructions and diagrams.

DRYING THE CHEESE. Most of the hard cheeses require a little extra time sitting at room temperature after pressing. Cheeses such as Cheddar that do not grow mold can be waxed and stored for aging after being pressed.

As long as your kitchen is cool and clean, it is okay to leave the cheese out in the open as pictured.

WAXING THE CHEESE. Some cheeses, to protect the rind and hold in moisture require that they be waxed. By slowly heating cheese wax in a saucepot, it can be melted and spread over the cheese with a small pastry brush. Be sure to apply at least two coats. Once the wax cools and solidifies, the cheese is ready to be aged. Use only cheese wax available at supply stores, the standard paraffin wax available in grocery stores will crack and does not work well.

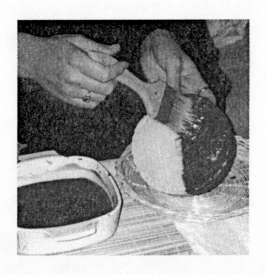

AGING THE CHEESE. Making cheese is like making a fine wine. A little age means a more intense, smooth flavor. For mold-ripened cheeses, this is the time that the mold imparts its specific flavor and grows throughout the cheese.

Preparing Your Own Starter Culture

Ingredients and Equipment
1 Quart of Skim Milk
2 pint jars or 1 quart jar (Mason style) with lids, sterilized
1 package (or ½ teaspoon) of freeze-dried starter culture
(Do not use "Direct-Set" powders as these contain rennet.)

Pour the skim milk into each jar, leaving about ½ inch space from the top. Cover each jar tightly with the lids. Place the jars in a large pot with just enough water to cover the tops. Heat the water to a boil and let simmer for at least 30 minutes. Remove the jars and allow to cool.

If you are making a Thermophillic starter, allow the milk to cool until it reaches 108°-110°F. If making a Mesophilic starter, keep cooling the milk until it drops to 70°-72°F. Measure the temperature with your dairy thermometer to make sure that the temperatures are correct.

Once the milk reaches the desired temperature, open the jars and add the freeze-dried culture. Close the jars again quickly and swirl them for a minute or two to make sure that they are mixed thoroughly.

Place the jars in a draft-free area where the temperature will remain near 72°. Allow the jars to ripen for 20-24 hours.

To see if the culture is ready, open the jars. The culture should be thick, much like yogurt and will separate from the sides of the jar cleanly. The culture will have a tangy, but sweet taste. Once ready, use right away or store in the refrigerator or freeze. Starter cultures will last 2-3 days in the refrigerator and up to three months frozen.

To freeze your culture, fill four sterilized ice cube trays with the culture. Place in the freezer until they are hard. Once frozen, break out the cubes and place in an airtight plastic bag and back in the freezer for storage.

Each ice cub will be approximately one ounce, which you can use in your cheese recipes, or use to make more starter culture. When making more starter culture, add two cubes of starter instead of freeze-dried powder and prepare the same way. Remember to allow them to thaw before using. This'll save time and money since you will not have to buy more starter and can keep making more when needed.

Let's Get Started

I hope you decide to make all of the cheeses in this book and discover a few new favorites that you can share with family and friends. There is great joy in making a fine cheese and surprising your guests when you tell them that you made that wonderful Stilton or Cheddar in your own kitchen. Once that fact has been discovered, you will be talking about cheese all night, so be prepared to give a speech and possibly to show how it is done. In this book, you will find many familiar cheeses such as Cottage, Cheddar and Mozzarella along with some unfamiliar names.

It is best to start with some of the easier cheeses until you gain a feel for the entire process. Starting with a very difficult cheese such as Danish Blue will only cause frustration if it doesn't turn out just right the first time. The mold and age-ripened cheeses take a considerable investment in time to ripen fully. Remember, practice makes perfect. Start with a cream or cottage cheese, and then try a slightly more difficult cheese like Mozzarella before tackling the more time consuming hard cheeses. The softer cheeses are much easier to make, and many can be eaten right away.

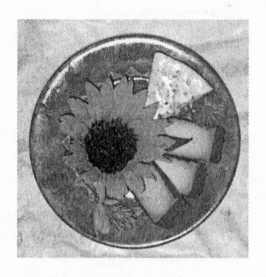

Once you feel like a pro making the easier cheeses, slowly venture into the world of mold or age ripened cheeses. Your experience in making the softer cheeses will ensure that your attempts at making more difficult cheeses are a success the first time. Making cheese is a lot like learning to drive a car or fly a plane; you can learn everything you need to know from a book, but you actually have to practice to be able to "feel" how to drive or fly. The softer cheeses give you the practice that you need to "feel" how to make great cheeses. With enough practice, you will simply know if your cheese is progressing smoothly.

Soft Cheeses

Soft cheeses are not only fun and easy to make, but they can be eaten right away. Soft cheeses are not pressed, do not require a lot of equipment and are excellent for the beginning cheese maker.

Because they are not pressed, soft cheeses contain a large percentage of water. They can be kept for one to two weeks in the refrigerator. This chapter revolves around two types of soft cheeses, "bagged" cheeses and "cottage" cheeses. These cheeses differ in the method used to drain off excess whey. Bagged cheeses are hung in a "bag" of cheesecloth to allow whey to drain away for a few hours. Cottage cheeses are simply drained for just a few minutes in a cheesecloth-lined colander.

Soft cheeses have a higher moisture content than hard cheeses which means they feel wet and will deteriorate rather quickly. These cheeses cannot be aged, as they will spoil within two weeks or less of being made.

The microbes that are present in these cheeses have not had a chance to change the milk sugars into lactic acid. Consequently, the flavor of these fresh cheeses remains very mild and sometimes slightly lemony or acidic.

A poet's hope: to be,
Like some valley cheese,
Local, but prized elsewhere.

W.H. Auden (1907-1973)

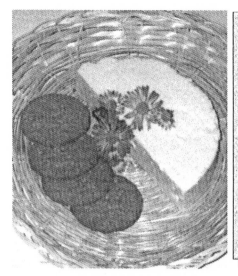

Queso Blanco

Difficulty
Easy

Time
4 hours to finish

Storage
Up to one week refrigerated

Weight
1 ½ to 2 pounds

Milk
Cow or Goat

Queso Blanco is a simple Latin American cheese popular in many Latin dishes, especially Mexican. It's name translates to "white cheese." It is a crumbly, moist cheese that acts quite like Cheddar for cooking. It's flavor is mild, almost bland and slightly sweet. Queso Blanco is the original Monterey Jack cheese. The massed produced Monterey Jack cheeses that most people are used to are more bland and rubbery than this original cheese. The name Jack cheese came from David Jacks, a Scotsman who was given credit for the cheese. However, the original Jack cheese, Queso Blanco can trace its roots farther back to Spanish Franciscan monks originally from Mexico.

Ingredients

1 gallon whole goat's or cow's milk
¼ cup cider vinegar

Heating

No double boiler is needed for this cheese. Heat the milk *slowly* on direct heat, stirring it frequently to prevent burning. Using a medium-low heat, stir and heat until the milk reaches a temperature of 180°F. Maintain the 180°F temperature for several minutes.

Acid Coagulation

After the 180°F temperature has been held for 10 minutes, slowly stir in the cider vinegar until the milk solidifies and small curds start to form.

Draining

Remove the pot from the heat. Drain the curds by pouring the whole mixture through a colander lined with cheesecloth to keep the curds from escaping. Tie a knot with the corners of the cheesecloth to form a bag of curds. Hang the bag over a pot for draining. The bag can be hung from a hook, or you may use chopsticks or spoons pushed through the knot to hold the bag on the sides of a pot to drain. Let the bag drain for 3-4 hours, until the bag stops dripping.

Storing

Open the bag and remove the solid mass of curds. They can be wrapped in a plastic wrap or stored in an airtight container in the refrigerator. This cheese can be eaten immediately, or stored for up to a week in the refrigerator.

Chevre

Difficulty
Easy

Time
24 hours to finish

Storage
Up to two weeks
refrigerated

Weight
1 to 1 ¼ pounds

Milk
Goat

Chevre is a thick and creamy cheese with a slight hint of acidity due to the goat's milk. Traditionally, many Chevre cheeses are covered in fresh tyme or tarragon, giving a beautiful contrast to the stark-white color of the cheese. With age, the texture turns creamier and is a family favorite, even for those who do not particularly like goat's milk cheeses.

Ingredients
     1 gallon raw (if available) whole goat's milk
     ¼ teaspoon salt
     1 packet of *direct-set* chevre starter culture

Heating

In a double boiler, slowly heat the milk to a temperature of 170°F while stirring frequently. Once the milk reaches 170°F, remove the milk and plunge into a sink or vat half-filled with cold water and ice. Keep the ice water cold by adding more ice or replacing the cold water constantly. The object is to reduce the temperature of the milk quickly now that it has been pasteurized. Bring the temperature of the milk down to at least 72°F.

Ripening

Once cooled to 72°F, slowly stir in the *direct-set* starter culture. These cultures include not only the bacteria required to ripen the cheese, but also contain the rennet necessary to coagulate the milk into curds quickly. Make sure your starter culture packet is measured for one gallon of milk as called for in this recipe. Cover the pot with a towel and leave it in a draft-free place. Allow the cheese to set for at least 12 hours. When ready, the curds will form a thick consistency, much like a thick yogurt.

Line your stainless-steel colander with cheesecloth. If you have a cheese mold to use for your chevre, the cheesecloth is not needed. With a ladle, spoon the curds into the lined colander or cheese mold. Cover with an extra piece of cheesecloth and allow to rest and drain for about 8 hours.

Transfer your solid cheese into a bowl and sprinkle the salt over the cheese. This cheese can be served immediately or stored in an airtight container for up to 2 weeks.

Cream Cheese

Difficulty
Easy

Time
40 hours to finish

Storage
Up to one week
refrigerated

Weight
About 10 oz.

Milk
Cow milk & cream

This cheese is a year-round favorite due to its creamy texture and many uses. Once the cheese is ready, your favorite herbs, spices or fruit can be added for a special treat. This cheese can be used in recipes or served as a spread for a wonderful breakfast.

Ingredients

3 cups whole cow's milk
3 cups whipping cream
2 oz. Mesophilic culture (or ½ tsp. Powdered)
2 drops of rennet

Heating

Whisk together the milk and cream in your double boiler. Slowly warm the milk to a temperature of just 72°F. Remove the pot from the stove and set aside.

Ripening

Pour the starter into the milk and stir until it is thoroughly combined. Add the rennet and stir it into the mixture to combine well. Cover your pot and set in a draft-free place. Allow the mixture to ripen undisturbed for 24 hours. The mixture will resemble yogurt.

Line your stainless steel colander with cheesecloth and set in a basin to drain. Slowly pour or ladle your cheese mixture into the colander. Pull up the ends of the cheesecloth and knot them to make a bag for hanging. Hang the bag over a pot for draining. The bag can be hung from a hook, or you may use chopsticks or spoons pushed through the knot to hold the bag on the sides of a pot to drain. Let the curds drain for 12 hours until the whey no longer drips and you have a solid mass of cheese.

Storing

Spoon the curds into a bowl with an airtight lid. Stir the curds until they are again creamy. You can add your fruit or herbs to the mixture now and allow the flavors to blend into the cheese by letting sit in the refrigerator for an hour.

Neufchatel

Difficulty
　　Moderate

Time
　　48 hours to finish

Storage
　　Up to one week
　　refrigerated

Weight
　　About 2 pounds

Milk
　　Cow milk & cream

As you may have guessed from the name, Neufchatel is a French cheese, specifically from the Normandy region. Unlike other soft cheeses, this one is lightly pressed to remove extra moisture. Typically, Neufchatel is quite grainy and has a slightly bitter taste. As shown in this picture, it is delicious when rolled in herbs such as mint, parsley or sage.

Ingredients
　　1 gallon whole milk
　　1 pint of heavy cream

4 ounces of mesophilic starter culture, or 1 teaspoon powdered starter culture

1 teaspoon of diluted rennet (see recipe)

Heating

In your double boiler, mix the milk and cream
thoroughly and heat slowly to 72°F. Cover and set
aside while you prepare the rennet solution.

Ripening and Renneting

Add just three drops of liquid rennet to 1/3 cup of
cool sterile water. This is an important step and the
amount of rennet and water must be exact. Stir in
your mesophilic starter culture to the milk and add
just one teaspoon of the rennet/water mix you just
made. Cover the milk mixture and let sit in a draft
free place for 12 to 18 hours or until a thick curd has
formed.

Draining

Pour the curds into a cheesecloth-lined colander.
Pull up the ends of the cheesecloth and knot them to
make a bag for hanging. Hang the bag over a pot for
draining. The bag can be hung from a hook, or you
may use chopsticks or spoons pushed through the
knot to hold the bag on the sides of a pot to drain.
Let the curds drain for 6 to 12 hours until the whey
no longer drips and you have a solid mass of cheese.

Take the curds down and place into a cheesecloth-lined colander. Place the colander in another larger pot. Place a plate or round cutting board on top of the curds and weigh down with a gallon jug of water or other weight. Cover the whole pot and refrigerate for 12 hours.

Salting and Storing

Remove the cheese from the pot and cheesecloth and place in a bowl. Because of the large cheese that is made from this recipe, you can divide the cheese into three or four separate cheeses. Salt each to your taste and mold into any shape you wish. The cheese can be eaten now or wrapped in plastic wrap and kept in the refrigerator for up to a week.

Cottage

Difficulty
   Easy

Time
   24 hours to finish

Storage
   Up to one week
   refrigerated

Weight
   1 ½ pounds

Milk
   Cow's milk

Cottage cheese is one of the most popular cheeses in the world originating in Europe. It is a soft, cooked curd cheese that is eaten fresh. This version, made at home has an extra tang that is missing from commercial cheeses, which are highly processed and contain unwanted ingredients like preservatives and flavor additives and gums. This cheese can be served plain or add tomatoes or fruit to make a tasty lunch.

Ingredients

> 1 gallon whole cow's milk
> 4 tablespoons heavy cream
> 4 ounces fresh starter culture, or ½ teaspoon mesophilic powdered starter culture
> ¼ teaspoon salt

Heating

In your double boiler, slowly heat the milk until it reaches a temperature of 72°F.

Adding Starter

Stir in the starter culture into the milk thoroughly. Cover the pot and remove from the stove. Place the pot into a draft-free area where the temperature of the curds will remain around 72°F. Allow the curds to form overnight, at least 15 hours. The curd will be firm, but not hard.

Cutting and Stirring the Curds

With your stainless-steel curd knife, gently cut the curds into ½ inch cubes. Once cut, leave the curds alone for 30 minutes to allow them to drain slightly. The curds will sink to the bottom of the pot and whey will form at the top.

Place the pot of curds back onto the stove to heat very slowly. The curds will need to be heated to a temperature of 110°F. Be sure to heat the curds very slowly so that the whole process takes about 45 minutes. This means that the curds should not rise more than three or four degrees for every five minutes that passes. At each 5-minute mark, stir the curds carefully to prevent them from sticking to each other.

Once the cheese reaches 110°F, keep the temperature constant for 30 minutes. During this process, the curds will shrink and firm as they release even more whey. Spoon out a few curds and squeeze them to check for the right firmness. The curds should be springy and should not be mushy. If your curds are still mushy, leave on the stove and continue cooking for an additional 10 minutes.

Once the curds are sufficiently cooked, remove the pot from the heat and allow the curds to settle again.

Draining

Line your stainless steel colander with cheesecloth and place it in an empty pot to hold the whey as it drains. Slowly pour the curds into the colander and allow to drain for an extra 10 minutes.

Washing the Curds

Fill a bowl with cold, fresh water. Pull up the corners of the cheesecloth to form a bag and dip it into the bowl a few times. Allow the cheese to drain for an additional 15 minutes.

Storing

Spoon your curds into a large bowl and stir the curds gently with a fork to loosen them. Add the heavy cream and stir into the curds. Sprinkle the salt into your cottage cheese and stir again. Pour your cottage cheese into an airtight container and refrigerate for an hour before serving. Cottage cheese will stay fresh for a week when refrigerated.

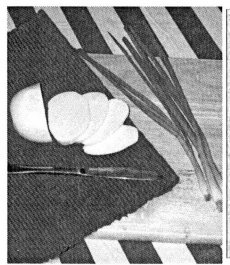

Mozzarella

Difficulty
Moderate

Time
24 hours to finish

Storage
Up to one week
refrigerated

Weight
1 pound

Milk
Cow or Goat

Many cheese lovers believe that the best mozzarellas in the world are made from buffalo. That's a neat fact, but doesn't help those of us who don't live near a buffalo herd. This recipe is formulated to produce a wonderful mozzarella from cow's milk, but goat's milk can also be used for a different flavor experience. This is not the same semi-dry mozzarella style cheese that is used on pizzas. That mozzarella style cheese is made specifically for pizzas and is extra stringy and stretchy. This cheese is moister, tastes fresher and is great for baking.

Ingredients

    1 gallon whole cow or goat's milk

    1 ¼ teaspoons of citric acid powder dissolved in ¼ cup of water

    1 teaspoon liquid rennet, or ¼ crushed rennet tablet

    ¼ cup of water

    1/3 cup of cheese salt

    pH test strips for testing acidity

Heating

    In your stainless steel double boiler, heat the milk to 90°F. Once the milk reaches 90°F, spoon out a sample and test the pH for acidity. The reading on the test strip should be at or very close to 8.6pH.

Adding Acid and Rennet

    Stir in the dissolved citric acid mixture and blend in with a whisk. Let the mixture stand for 45 minutes on a warm stove, keeping the temperature at 90°F. Dissolve the crushed ¼ rennet tablet, or liquid into the ¼ cup of water. Add the rennet to the milk mixture and stir again. Remove the pot from the stove and cover.

Ripening

    Allow the covered pot to sit in a draft free place fro 90 minutes to allow the acid and rennet to work on the mixture. The curd will be finished ripening when it has a consistency of a thick yogurt.

Cutting the Curd

Cut the curds into 1 ½ inch cubes. With your long curd knife, cut once more along a diagonal to the bottom of the pot. Allow the curds to settle for an additional half hour. The curds will settle to the bottom of the pot and fresh whey will gather at the top.

Testing Acidity

Spoon out a sample of the whey and dip in another pH test strip. The pH strip should read close to 6.5pH. If it does not, let the curd rest awhile longer and test again until you reach 6.5pH.

Cooking the Curd

Return your double boiler to the stove and slowly increase the heat until the temperature reaches 100°F. This must be done very slowly, over the span of an hour or so. Make sure that the temperature of the curds and whey doesn't increase more than 2 degrees every five minutes. If the curds are heated any faster, they will not coagulate properly. Stir the curds just once or twice during the heating process to keep them separated. Once 100°F is reached, remove from the stove and allow the curds to rest for 10 more minutes.

Draining

Move the pot of curds to a sink of warm water (100°F) to allow the curds to acidify further. The whey will continue to separate from the curds. After 30 minutes, spoon off the whey using your ladle and turn (flip) the curds over. Repeat this spooning and flipping process for the next 2 ½ hours. Make sure to keep replacing the warm water around your pot to help keep the curds at or near 100°F.

After the 2 ½ hours have elapsed and the curds have been flipped 5 times, spoon out some whey and again test for acidity. Your reading should be about 5.3pH. If it is above this reading, keep the curds in the warm water bath until a reading of 5.3pH is reached.

Finishing the Mozzarella

On the stove, heat 2 quarts of water in a stainless steel pot to a temperature of 170°F and stir in the salt. Keep this salt solution at 170°F, no higher.

Remove your curds from the double boiler and place onto a cutting board or other sterile surface you can work on. With your knife, cut the curd into ½ slices, turn and cut again at ½ inch intervals to form ½ inch cubes. Dump the cubes into your stainless steel pot of warm salt water.

Take two wooden spoons and squeeze together a ball of curds. Knead the ball of curds with the spoons until smooth and round. After a few minutes of kneading, pull at a corner of the ball of cheese. It should be stretchy and shiny. Keep working the ball of cheese until the whey turns cloudy and small blisters form on the surface of the cheese.

Cooling the Mozzarella

Drop the ball of cheese into a bowl of cold water and allow to rest for a few minutes. Remove from the bowl and transfer to a bowl of salt solution made from ½ gallon of cool water and 2 cups of salt. Leave the ball of cheese in the salt solution for 8 to 10 hours (overnight).

Storing

Remove the mozzarella from the salt solution and serve immediately, or store in an airtight container in the refrigerator. Fresh mozzarella will keep well for a week when refrigerated or as long as a couple of months if frozen.

Whey Ricotta

Difficulty
  Moderate

Time
  4 hours to finish

Storage
  Up to one week
  refrigerated

Weight
  1 ½ cups

Milk
  Cow or Goat whey

Ricotta is Italian for "re-cooked" or "twice cooked" and is made from whey that is usually discarded after making other cheeses. When making another cheese from this book, try and save the whey to make this cheese. Make sure that the whey is fresh, no more than an hour old and still warm. Ricotta is delicious when combined with fruit and herbs and is used extensively in baking in foods such as lasagna and stuffed pastas.

Ingredients
    2 gallons of fresh whey
    ¼ cup of heavy cream

¼ cup cider vinegar
Salt to taste

Heating and Ripening the Whey

Pour the whey into a large stainless steel pot and heat directly over the stove burner until it reaches 200°F. Once the temperature is right, stir in the cider vinegar and remove the pot from the heat. Small pieces of curd will slowly float to the top of the whey.

Draining

Pour the curds and whey into a colander lined with cheesecloth. Pull up the ends of the cheesecloth and knot them to make a bag for hanging. Hang the bag over a pot for draining. The bag can be hung from a hook, or you may use chopsticks or spoons pushed through the knot to hold the bag on the sides of a pot to drain. Let the curds drain for 3 to 4 hours until the whey no longer drips and you have a solid mass of cheese.

Serving and Storing

Remove the bag from the pot and spoon the curds into a bowl. Stir in the cream and salt to taste. Serve immediately, or store in an airtight container in your refrigerator.

Cream Ricotta

Difficulty
Moderate

Time
2 hours

Storage
Up to one week
refrigerated

Weight
1 pound

Milk
Cow milk & cream

Cream ricotta is a favorite for baking and is used extensively in making lasagna, manicotti and other stuffed pastas. Cream ricotta, as its name suggests is creamier than whey ricotta, has a bland yet semi-sweet taste.

Ingredients
½ gallon whole cow's milk
1 cup of heavy cream
¼ teaspoon salt
1/3 cup fresh lemon juice

Heating

Stir the milk, cream and lemon juice together in a small stainless steel pot. Heat slowly for 45 minutes until it reaches a temperature of 165°F. Stir the mixture just once or twice while heating to prevent burning. Make sure that the mixture is heated slowly, no more than 10°F every 5 minutes. Small curds will start to form as the milk heats.

Increase the heat on the formed curds and whey and warm for another 10 minutes until they reach 200°F. The whey will be on the verge of boiling. As long as the heat stays near 200°F, the curds will form a soft texture.

Draining the Curds

Remove the pot from the stove and allow to rest and cool for 15 minutes. During this time, the curds will sink to the bottom of the pot.

Line your stainless steel colander with thick cheesecloth. Spoon the curds with your ladle into the colander and allow to drain for an additional 15 to 20 minutes.

Serving and Storing

When drained, the curds should remain smooth and creamy. Stir in the salt and serve immediately, or store in an airtight container, refrigerated for up to a week.

Mascarpone

Difficulty
    Easy

Time
    12 hours to finish

Storage
    Up to two weeks
    refrigerated

Weight
    1 ½ cups

Milk
    Light Cream

Mascarpone (sometimes spelled Mascherpone) is a delightfully sweet cheese that is wonderful eaten straight from a bowl. Although it looks like a thick and grainy sour cream, its sweetness makes for a wonderful dessert when mixed with fresh fruit. Mascarpone is one of the main ingredients in tiramisu, the famous Italian dessert.

Ingredients
    1 quart light cream
    ¼ teaspoon tartaric acid

Heating

Slowly heat the cream in your double boiler over a moderate to low heat. Slowly warm the cream (light cream, not heavy cream) until the temperature reaches 175°F. Lower the heat at this point to maintain the cream's temperature without raising it. Sprinkle in the tartaric acid and blend thoroughly with a whisk.

The cream should start to thicken almost immediately and continue until it reaches the consistency of a custard or thick pudding. If the cream does not coagulate after a few minutes of stirring, add an extra pinch of tartaric acid. Cook the cream for a total of about 5 minutes.

Draining the Curd

Line a stainless steel colander with cheesecloth. Spoon the curds into the colander and allow to drain for about one hour. Place the colander into a bowl and allow to continue draining in the refrigerator for an additional 10-12 hours.

Storing

Once drained, transfer the cheese into an airtight container for storage under refrigeration. The cheese will stay fresh for up to two weeks before starting to sour.

Hard Cheeses

Once you've tried your hand at making one or two soft cheeses, it's time to move on to some of the more difficult, but more rewarding hard cheeses. These cheeses require extra steps and most require additional aging time, so plan accordingly.

Because they are pressed, hard cheeses contain a smaller percentage of water. They can be kept several weeks in the refrigerator after cutting if wrapped tightly in plastic wrap. These cheeses are placed in a mold where they are pressed after draining. The mold presses out extra water and makes a firm, sliceable cheese.

These cheeses can be aged for several months to intensify their flavor. Because of the long aging time, the bacterial cultures in the cheese have had time to impart their flavor in the cheese.

"How can you govern a country
Which has 246 varieties of cheese?"

Charles DeGaulle (1890-1970)

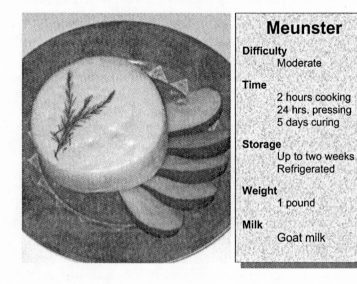

Meunster

Difficulty
Moderate

Time
2 hours cooking
24 hrs. pressing
5 days curing

Storage
Up to two weeks
Refrigerated

Weight
1 pound

Milk
Goat milk

Muenster is one of the world's most popular cheeses. Its mild flavor marries well with other ingredients in recipes although it is also delicious all by itself. This recipe calls for goat's milk, but it can also be prepared using whole cow's milk if you prefer. Using cow's milk gives this cheese a lighter flavor; more similar to the Muenster cheeses you are familiar with from your local supermarket.

Ingredients
    1 gallon whole goat's (or cow's) milk
    ¼ teaspoon rennet diluted in ¼ cup of water
    2 teaspoons salt

Heating and Renneting the Milk

Using your double boiler, heat the milk slowly until it reaches a temperature of 88°F to 90°F. Remove the pot from the burner and allow to rest for 5 minutes.

Dilute the liquid rennet in 2 ounces (1/4 cup) of water and add the mixture to the warmed milk. Use a whisk to thoroughly mix in the rennet, cover your pot and allow the rennet to work undisturbed for 1 hour. When whey has risen to the top of the pot and the curd has thickened enough to break cleanly from the sides of the pot when tested, you are ready to cut the curd.

Using your curd knife, cut the curd into 1-inch square cubes. Make sure to cut all the way to the bottom of the pot. Sprinkle the curds with the salt. Move the double boiler back to the stove and warm using a low heat. Using a large spoon, slowly turn the curds. Try not to stir vigorously as this will cause the curds to break into pieces that are too small. Just turn the curds to mix in the salt and allow to rest again.

Draining and Pressing the Curds

Pour or spoon the curds into a cheesecloth-lined colander and allow to drain for 20-25 minutes.

Once complete, spoon the curds into a cheese-press mold lined with fresh cheesecloth. Apply about

40 pounds of pressure to the curds and allow to press undisturbed for 12 hours. Remove your cheese, flip over and reapply the same amount of pressure for another 12 hours.

Curing the Cheese

After removing the Muenster from the cheese-cloth, rub the surface lightly with salt, place it on a cheese mat and cover the very top of the cheese with a plate or lid from a pot.

Each day for the next 5 or 6 days, salt all sides of the cheese, and turn over. After a few days, the cheese will form a soft rind and will firm slightly. After a rind has formed, the cheese is ready to be eaten.

Cheddar

Difficulty
    Moderate

Time
    8 hrs. preparation
    1 day pressing
    45 days aging

Storage
    Several weeks
    refrigerated

Weight
    About 2 pounds

Milk
    Whole cow's milk

Cheddar is one of the most popular cheeses in the world, especially in America. Originally produced in England in the 1500's, Cheddar is names after the town in England where it was invented. With a golden color and a sharp tang that occurs with aging, Cheddar is great with crackers, by itself, or with fruit. Cheddar is made by slicing the curds and allowing them to set before pressing. The addition of liquid annatto cheese coloring gives Cheddar cheeses their golden color. Using liquid annatto is optional. If you do not use annatto, you will still produce wonderful "white" Cheddar.

Ingredients

> 2 galloons of whole cow's milk
> Liquid annatto coloring
> 4 tablespoons of fresh starter culture or ½ teaspoon mesophilic starter powder
> 1 teaspoon of liquid rennet diluted in ½ cup of water
> Cheese wax

Heating and Ripening the Milk

Heat the milk in your double boiler over low heat until it reaches 85°F. Slowly stir in the starter culture (either dry starter powder or your fresh starter culture). Remove the mixture from the heat, cover and let set and ripen for at least one hour.

If you would like to make yellow Cheddar, add the liquid annatto now. Liquid annatto is very strong and only a small amount is needed. Add no more than 4 or 5 drops. Stir the annatto into the milk mixture thoroughly. The light yellow color that you see will get darker after we add the rennet, so resist the temptation to add more at this point.

Adding Rennet to the Cheese

After adding your color and allowing the cheese to set for an additional 5-10 minutes, it is time to use rennet. Stir the rennet into a ½ cup of fresh water to dilute and pour into the milk mixture. Stir thoroughly, cover and allow the rennet to work for 1 hour. When the curd breaks cleanly from the side of the pot when tested, you are ready to proceed. Cut the curd into ½" cubes using your curd knife and allow to rest for 5 minutes.

Cooking and Draining the Curds

After the curds have set, return your double boiler to the stove over low heat. Since the curd has set, it is important to heat them slowly to avoid burning. Heat slowly until the temperature of the curds reaches 100°F. This process should take at least half an hour, so use a low heat.

Using a large spoon, turn the curds occasionally while heating to 100°F. Once this temperature has been reached, hold the temperature at 100°F for half an hour. Occasionally turn the curds during this time. After half an hour has passed, remove the curds from the stove and allow them to settle to the bottom of the pot.

Pour the curds into a cheesecloth-lined colander and allow to drain for 20 minutes.

Cheddaring

This step is what separates Cheddar cheese from any other. In this step, the curds will be sliced and soaked in water before being cut into cubes.

To begin the cheddaring process, place the whole mass of curds onto a cutting board or large plate. The curds should be one large mass that sticks together. If they do not stick together, they were heated to quickly and will not produce a quality Cheddar cheese. You can still continue, but remember to be more careful the next time.

Cut the curds into ½ inch slices, like you would slice bread. Move the slices of curds back to the double boiler and keep warm in a sink of warm water. Keep the surrounding sink water warm to the touch (100°F to 105°F) for two hours, turning the sliced curds over every 30 minutes.

After about two hours, the curds will firm slightly and will be springy to the touch. Using your curd knife, cut the curds into ¾ inch cubes. Return the pot to the warm water and occasionally turn the curds while they are kept warm for 45 minutes. The curds will harden and expel additional whey.

Salting and Pressing the Curds

Remove the pot from the warm water and sprinkle the curds with the salt. Stir the curds to thoroughly distribute the salt. Spoon the curds into a cheese mold lined with fresh cheesecloth. Fold the top of the cheesecloth over to cover all exposed areas and apply 40 pounds of pressure for 12 straight hours. Flip the cheese and apply pressure for an additional 12 hours. Do this once more so that the cheese is pressed for at least 36 hours.

Remove the cheese from the press and from the cheesecloth. Place the cheese onto your cheese mat and allow it to dry in the open air for 3 days. Remember to turn over once each day.

Aging Your Cheese

Now that the cheese has had time to dry, the aging process can begin. If you cannot wait for your cheese to be aged, it can be eaten now. However, if you have the patience, and aged Cheddar is well worth the wait.

To prevent your Cheddar from drying when aging, it must be waxed. Heat a brick of cheese wax in a small saucepan over low heat until melted. Using a new, high-quality craft paintbrush, paint all surfaces of the cheese with the melted wax. The wax will solidify almost immediately, but it will be hot, so use care when applying. Once completely covered and coated with at least two applications, move your cheese to the refrigerator where it can be held at about 55°F. If you can remember, turn the Cheddar once a day for 3 to 12 months. This will prevent dry spots and guarantee a delicious cheese that you can be proud of.

Variations

Sage Cheddar

Once you try Sage Cheddar, you will be hooked forever. It is one of our family's favorites. You may wish to attempt other versions using herbs such as parsley or even chives. Making Sage Cheddar involves just a few more minutes of work, but the results are well worth your effort.

Preparing and Adding the Sage

Simmer ½ cup of water in a small saucepan and add ¼ to 1/3 cup of Sage. Simmer for 5 minutes. Remove the pan from the stove and allow to cool.

Drain off the water and add to the milk at the start of this recipe. Add the sage to the cheese at the same time you add the salt.

Hot-Pepper Cheddar

Hot-pepper cheeses are very popular, especially with the rise of the spicy dishes of Latin America. The simple addition of jalapeno or red peppers to this recipe will add a touch of fire to your cheese and bring out the smiles of friends and family. This cheese is especially good served sliced with crackers, or grated on spicy dishes.

Preparing and Adding the Pepper

In a small saucepan, boil one cup of water and add 1 to 2 teaspoons of dried, crushed jalapeno or red pepper (or 1 to 4 tablespoons of chopped, fresh peppers). Simmer the pepper for at least 10 minutes. Drain off the water and add it to the milk prior to starting your cheese for an extra kick. Add the cooked pepper to the curds at the same time you add the salt.

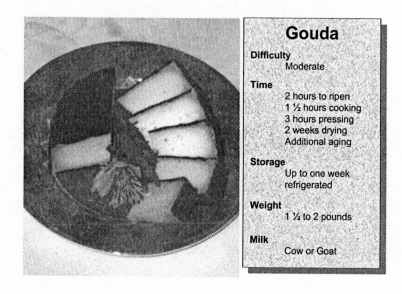

Gouda

Difficulty
Moderate

Time
2 hours to ripen
1 ½ hours cooking
3 hours pressing
2 weeks drying
Additional aging

Storage
Up to one week
refrigerated

Weight
1 ½ to 2 pounds

Milk
Cow or Goat

Gouda is Holland's best-known cheese. Coated in cheese wax, it is mild, smooth and pale yellow. Gouda ages well, and certain Goudas from Holland are aged over three years. Gouda's creamy texture marries well with fruit or crackers and is used extensively in cooking. This Gouda is not quite like the store-bought Goudas. It has much more flavor and is much creamier. Gouda is a "washed-curd" cheese. This means that the extra whey is drained from the curds and is replaced with fresh water to "wash" the curds. I am quite sure you will enjoy this cheese.

Ingredients

2 gallons of whole cow or goat's milk

1 teaspoon liquid rennet diluted in ½ cup of water

8 tablespoons (½ cup) fresh mesophilic starter culture or 1 packet dry mesophilic powder

1 gallon of brine solution (4 cups of salt dissolved in 1 gallon of water)

Cheese wax

Heating and Ripening the Milk

In your double boiler, heat the 2 gallons of milk over a medium-low heat for 30 minutes until the milk reaches 90°F. Add your mesophilic starter culture (either fresh or dry) and stir until thoroughly blended.

Dissolve 1 teaspoon of liquid rennet into ½ cup of cool water. With a slotted spoon or whisk, stir in the rennet solution until mixed completely. Remove your pot from the stove, cover and allow to ripen for at least 2 hours.

Test the curd with your knife. If the curd pulls away from the side of the pot cleanly, they are ready for cooking. If the curd is still not quite solid and sticks to your knife, allow it to set for an additional 30 minutes.

Cut the curd into ½" cubes using your curd knife and allow to rest for 5 minutes.

Cooking the Curd

Place the curds back onto the stove over medium-low heat. Slowly raise the temperate until the curd reaches 100°F. This process should take at least a half hour, so make sure that the curds do not heat more than 2°F every 5 minutes.

Rinsing the Curd

Once the curd reaches 100°F, dip a measuring cup into the whey that has risen to the top and scoop out of your pot. Remove all whey that you can from the top of the curd. Remember to measure how much whey that you have removed as you will replace the whey with an exact amount of fresh water of the same temperature (100°F). Each time to make Gouda, the amount of whey that you remove will vary slightly. On average, you will remove about 6 cups, sometimes more, sometimes less.

Using a slotted spoon, turn the water into the curds. After a few minutes, the curds will absorb much of the fresh warm water. Continue turning the curds every few minutes to release even more whey until about 10 minutes has elapsed.

Repeat this entire process of rinsing the curds at least three times. Once completed, drain off any remaining whey and water and allow the curds to settle for 15 minutes.

Pressing the Cheese

Line your cheese mold with fresh cheesecloth and spoon the curd into the mold. Fold the cheesecloth over the top to make sure that no curds show through. Apply 15 pounds of pressure to the cheese for ½ hour. Flip the Gouda and return the pressure for another 30 minutes. Flip once more and return the pressure for another 30 minutes.

Brining and Drying

After pressing, remove the cheese form the mold and remove the cheesecloth. Mix the 4 cups of salt into 1 gallon of fresh water to create a brining solution. Place the cheese in this solution and allow to float for 2 to 3 hours. Flip the cheese over every half hour during this process.

Remove the cheese, pat dry and place on your cheese mat or plate for drying. Move the cheese to the refrigerator and allow to air dry for 2 to three weeks. Turn the cheese daily to ensure that a smooth rind will form around the cheese.

Waxing and Aging the Cheese

Prepare the cheese wax as described in the Cheddar recipe. Coat the Gouda with the wax using a new craft or barbeque sauce brush. Move the coated cheese back into the refrigerator and allow to age for 3 to 6 months. The perfect temperature to age Gouda is around 50°F. If your refrigerator is cooler than this temperature, the cheese will not be quite as creamy, but will still be delicious. It is possible to age the Gouda for 9 to 12 months, but it takes a strong will to wait that long. Flip the cheese over every few days to ensure that it cures evenly, without any dry or hard spots.

Variations

Hot-Pepper Gouda

This is one of those cheeses that were created in my kitchen on a whim. I am a fan of cheeses with hot peppers used in the recipe, but have never seen a commercial Gouda cheese using peppers. This extra step will guarantee a cheese that your pepper-loving friends and family will devour.

In a small saucepan, boil one cup of water and add 1 to 2 teaspoons of dried, crushed jalapeno or red pepper (or 1 to 4 tablespoons of chopped, fresh peppers). Simmer the pepper for at least 10 minutes. Drain off the water and add it to the milk prior to starting your cheese for extra flavor. Add the cooked pepper to the curds just prior to draining at the end of the "Rinsing the Curd" section of the recipe.

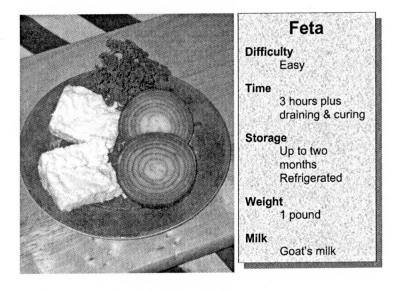

Feta

Difficulty
Easy

Time
3 hours plus
draining & curing

Storage
Up to two
months
Refrigerated

Weight
1 pound

Milk
Goat's milk

Feta is the most popular of the Greek cheeses and is quite common throughout the world. One of the most versatile of cheeses, it holds its shape when sautéed but crumbles easily. Feta is a highly salted cheese and is an essential ingredient in Greek salads.

Ingredients

1 gallon whole goat's milk

2 ounces mesophilic starter culture

1 teaspoon liquid rennet, or ¼ crushed rennet tablet

Flake salt for salting and brining

Heating and Ripening the Milk

Slowly heat the milk in your double boiler until it reaches a temperature of 85°F. Thoroughly whisk in the starter culture to distribute into the milk evenly. Remove the milk from the stove, cover and allow it to ripen for two hours.

After the milk has ripened, dissolve the rennet into ¼ cup of cool water and pour into the ripened milk. Stir the mixture with a whisk again to make sure that the rennet is mixed throughout. Cover the pot again and allow to ripen for an additional 1 to 2 hours until the curd breaks cleanly from the side of the pot.

Cutting and Draining the Curds

With your long curd knife, cut the curds into ½ cubes, making sure to cut all the way to the bottom of the pot. Allow the cut curds to rest for 20 minutes. Stir the curds gently to break them up and cut any curds larger than ½ inch. For the next 30 minutes, stir again every few minutes while keeping the temperature near 85°F.

Spoon the curds into a cheesecloth-lined colander and allow to drain for just a few minutes. Tie the corners of the cheesecloth together to form a bad fro draining. Hang the bag inside the pot by inserting a skewer or chopsticks into the knot. Allow the bag of curds to drain for at least 5 hours. By this time, the curds should have stopped dripping and the curds should be firm to the touch. If they are still dripping or are still soft, allow to drain for an additional hour.

Curing the Cheese

Prepare a bowl of brine solution by mixing 1-½ cups of salt in 1 quart of warm water until the salt is completely dissolved. Place the bowl into your freezer until the brine is cold to the touch.

Remove the cheese from the cheesecloth bag and push into a tall, square container such as a Tupperware bowl. Place the cheese in your refrigerator to cool and harden. Remove the cheese from the container and cut into 1 inch cubes. Place the cubes into the bowl of cold brine solution. Allow the cheese to cure for at least 5 days in the brine. For a saltier cheese, allow the cubes to steep for up to 30 days. After brining, your cheese can be served immediately or refrigerated in an airtight container for up to 2 months.

Monterey Jack

Difficulty
Moderate

Time
4 hr. preparation
12 hr. pressing
3 months aging

Storage
Two weeks after
cutting

Weight
About 2 pounds

Milk
Cow's milk

The massed produced Monterey Jack cheeses that most people are used to are more bland and rubbery than the original cheese. The name Jack cheese came from David Jacks, a Scotsman who was given credit for inventing this cheese. This recipe stays true to the original recipe and is much more delicious than any of the store-bought versions.

Ingredients
2 gallons skim cow's milk
1 quart heavy cream
¼ teaspoon powdered Mesophilic starter culture
¼ teaspoon liquid rennet

½ teaspoon calcium chloride
1 tablespoon cheese salt

Heating and Ripening the Milk

Combine the skim milk and heavy cream in your double boiler.

Slowly heat the milk in your double boiler until it reaches a temperature of 88°F. Thoroughly whisk in the starter culture to distribute into the milk evenly. Remove the milk from the stove, cover and allow it to ripen for 45 minutes.

In a small glass bowl or measuring cup, dissolve the calcium chloride in ¼ cup of cool water. Add this mixture to the milk and stir gently to mix. Slowly increase the temperature of the milk mixture to 90°F.

Dissolve the rennet into ¼ cup of cool water and pour into the ripened milk. Stir the mixture with a whisk again to make sure that the rennet is mixed throughout. Cover the pot again and allow to ripen at 90°F for an additional 60 minutes or until the curd breaks cleanly from the side of the pot.

Cutting and Draining the Curds

With your long curd knife, cut the curds into ½ cubes, making sure to cut all the way to the bottom of the pot. Allow the cut curds to rest and drain for

15 minutes. Stir the curds very gently to break them up slightly.

Return your double boiler to the stove and slowly heat the curds and whey to a temperature of 100°F. Heat very slowly, increasing the temperature only 1-2°F every 5 minutes. Gently stir the curds every few minutes during this heating process.

Once you reach 100°F, maintain this temperature for an additional 30 minutes, stirring every few minutes.

Pour off the whey down to the level of the curds and place your pot into a warm bath in your kitchen sink. The water in the sink should be warm enough to maintain the curds at 100°F. You may need to add warm or cool water every few minutes to adjust. Maintain the 100°F temperature for 30 minutes.

Salting and Pressing the Curds

Pour the curds into a cheesecloth-lined colander in your sink to drain. Sprinkle the curds with the salt and gently mix to thoroughly distribute the salt. Spoon the curds into a cheese mold lined with fresh cheesecloth. Fold the top of the cheesecloth over to cover all exposed areas and apply 2 pounds of pressure for 30 minutes (a 1-quart milk jug full of water will work well). Flip the cheese and apply 4 pounds of pressure for an additional 12 hours.

Remove the cheese from the press and from the cheesecloth. Place the cheese onto your cheese mat and allow it to dry in the open air for 2 days. Remember to turn over once each day.

Waxing and Aging the Cheese

Prepare the cheese wax as described in the Cheddar recipe. Coat your cheese with the wax using your brush. Move the coated cheese back into the refrigerator and allow to age for 3 months. The perfect temperature to age Monterey Jack is around 45°F. If your refrigerator is cooler than this temperature, the cheese will not be quite as creamy, but will still be delicious. Remember to flip the waxed cheese over once each day for the first month.

Variations

Pepper Jack

Almost everyone who loves spicy foods has tried a store-bought Pepper Jack cheese. I honestly believe that once you make it yourself, you will never be able to buy that store-bought junk again!

In a small saucepan, boil one cup of water and add 1 to 2 teaspoons (or more… if you dare) dried, crushed jalapeno or red pepper (or 1 to 4 tablespoons of chopped, fresh peppers). Simmer the pepper for at least 10 minutes. Drain off the water and add it to the milk prior to starting your cheese for extra flavor. Add the cooked pepper to the curds just prior to draining at the end of the "Salting and Pressing the Curds" section of the recipe.

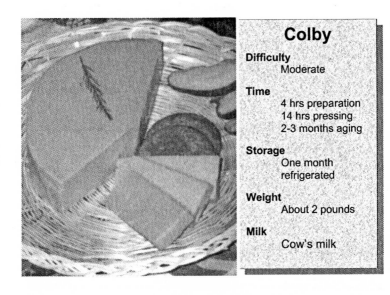

Colby

Difficulty
Moderate

Time
4 hrs preparation
14 hrs pressing
2-3 months aging

Storage
One month
refrigerated

Weight
About 2 pounds

Milk
Cow's milk

Colby is a style of Cheddar cheese in which the curds are washed during the cooking stage, much like the curds are washed when making Gouda. Colby is named after the town where it was invented in Wisconsin. Colby is slightly milder and softer than a standard Cheddar cheese. Once prepared, Colby can be aged for up to three months to bring out its full flavor.

Ingredients

2 gallons whole cow's milk
3 ounces mesophilic starter culture
1 teaspoon liquid rennet, or ¼ rennet tablet
2 tablespoons flake salt

Heating and Ripening the Milk

In your double boiler, warm two gallons of whole milk until it reaches a temperature of 86°F. Stir in the 3 ounces of mesophilic starter culture until mixed completely. Remove the milk from the stove, cover, and let ripen for 1 hour.

If you desire a stronger color to your Colby cheese, dissolve 4 or 5 drops of annatto cheese color into a ¼ cup of water and add to the milk at this stage. Annatto goes a long way; so do not add more than these few drops.

Renneting and Cutting the Curd

Dissolve 1 teaspoon of liquid rennet (or ¼ rennet tablet) in ¼ cup of cool water. Gently stir the dissolved rennet into the milk and slowly stir for a few minutes. Cover again and let set for 30 minutes, or until the curd breaks cleanly from the sides of the pot.

Using your long curd knife, cut the curd into ½ cubes. Stir the curds gently with your ladle to break them up. Let the curds rest for an additional 5 minutes before proceeding.

Cooking the Curd

Move the curds back to the stove and slowly warm until the temperature reaches 102°F. Make sure that the curds are warmed slowly, no more than 2°F every 5 minutes. Stir gently every few minutes so that the curds do not stick together. Once the curds reach 102°F, hold the temperature there for 30 minutes, stirring every few minutes.

Remove the pot from the stove and allow the curds to settle for 5 minutes, allowing them to settle to the bottom.

Draining and Washing the Curd

Drain off the extra whey, until the curds are just covered. Add cool tap water and stir until the temperature of the curds drops to 80°F. Stir the curds frequently and keep the temperature at a constant 80°F for 15 minutes. You may need to return the pot to a low-heat stove to maintain the temperature during this process.

Holding the temperature of the curd at 80°F will ensure a medium bodied cheese. If you prefer a dryer cheese, keep the curds a few degrees warmer than 80°F. If you prefer a moister cheese, let the curds cool to a few degrees under 80°F.

Pour the curds into a cheesecloth-lined colander and allow to drain for 20 minutes.

Salting and Pressing

Break up the curds into small pieces of about ½ inch. Add the flake salt and mix thoroughly, using your hands. Place the curd into a cheesecloth-lined mold. Press at 20 pounds of pressure for 20 minutes.

Flip the cheese over and press again using 30 pounds for an additional 20 minutes. Flip the cheese again and increase the pressure to 40 pounds for 20 minutes. Flip once more, and press at 50 pounds for 12 hours.

Drying and Pressing

Remove the cheese from the press and remove the cheesecloth. Allow to air-dry on a cheese mat or cheese board for 2 to 3 days.

Prepare the cheese wax as described in the Cheddar recipe. Coat the Colby with the wax using a new craft or barbeque sauce brush. Move the coated cheese back into the refrigerator (45°-50°F) and allow to age for 2 to 3 months, turning daily.

Romano

Difficulty
   Moderate

Time
   2 hrs preparation
   24 hrs pressing
   and brining
   6 months aging

Storage
   Several months
   refrigerated

Weight
   About 2 pounds

Milk
   Cow's milk

Romano is one of the world's oldest cheeses. It has been made near Rome for about 2,000 years. Like Parmesan, this cheese needs to be aged for at least 6 months to allow the full flavor to develop. Aging this cheese longer will produce a dryer cheese that is excellent for grating. Mixing goat and cow's milk in equal proportions can make a more flavorful cheese. In this recipe, capilase enzyme powder is used to increase that sharp flavor that Romano cheese is famous for. Using capilase is optional, but recommended and is available from most cheese supply stores listed in the back of this book.

Ingredients

2 gallons of 2% cow's milk

4 tablespoons thermophilic starter, or 1 teaspoon powdered

¾ teaspoon liquid rennet, or ¼ crushed rennet tablet

¼ teaspoon capilase enzyme powder (optional)

Salt brine solution

Heating and Ripening the Milk

Warm the milk in your double boiler over a medium heat until the milk reaches a temperature of 90°F. Remove the pot from the stove and slowly stir in the thermophilic starter. Cover the pot and allow the milk to ripen for 30 minutes.

Stir the capilase enzyme powder into ¼ cup of cool water until dissolved. Stir the capilase solution into the milk until mixed thoroughly. Dissolve the liquid rennet into ¼ cup of cool water and slowly stir into the milk. Cover and allow the rennet to work for 30 minutes, or until the curd breaks cleanly from the sides of the pot when tested.

Cutting and Cooking the Curd

Cut the curd with your long curd knife into ½ inch cubes and allow the curds to rest for 15 minutes.

Return the curds to the stove and slowly heat until the curds reach 115°F. This process should take about 45 minutes, stirring every few minutes. Hold the curds at 115°F for at least 10 minutes.

Draining and Pressing the Curds

Remove the pot from the stove and slowly pour into a cheesecloth-lined colander to drain the whey. Allow the curds to drain for 10 minutes.

Gently pour the drained curds into a cheesecloth lined mold and fold the cheesecloth over the top of the curds to completely cover.

Press the curds with 10 pounds of pressure for 20 minutes. Flip the curds and press for an additional 20 minutes.

Flip the curds and press at 20 pounds for 3 hours. Flip the curds once more and press at 35 pounds for 12 hours.

Brining, Drying and Curing the Cheese

Prepare a brine solution by dissolving 2 cups of salt into 2 quarts of cool water in a stainless-steel mixing bowl. After stirring vigorously, a small layer of salt will remain on the bottom of the pot.

Float the cheese into the brine solution for a total of 12 hours. Flip the cheese over every 3 to 4 hours to ensure an even rind develops.

Place the cheese in your refrigerator and allow to age for at least 6 months. Flip the cheese over once each day for the first two weeks, then weekly or it will dry unevenly. As most refrigerators keep the air too dry, cover your cheese with an overturned bowl after the first few days.

Inspect your cheese for mold every other day. If any surface mold develops, it can be removed by wiping with a paper towel soaked in vinegar. To help keep the cheese moist, rub the surface of the cheese with a small amount of olive oil after two weeks. This will help the cheese retain its moisture and help the natural rind formation.

Parmesan

Difficulty
    Moderate

Time
    2 days preparation
    6 months aging

Storage
    Several months
    when refrigerated

Weight
    About 2 pounds

Milk
    Cow or Goat

Named after an area in Italy called Parma, this is one of the world's most popular and widely enjoyed cheeses. While it is possible to make a good Parmesan style cheese using only cow's milk, using both cow and goat's milk will produce a much tastier cheese.

Ingredients
    1 gallon skim cow's milk
    1 gallon whole goat's milk
    4 ounces of fresh thermophilic starter culture, or
1 teaspoon powdered
    1 teaspoon liquid rennet, or ¼ crushed tablet

Heating the milk

Pour both the cow and goat's milk into your double boiler and slowly warm to a temperature of 90°F. Stir the thermophilic cheese starter into the milk mixture and hold the temperature at 90°F. Allow the milk mixture to ripen for 30 minutes.

Renneting the milk

Dissolve the rennet liquid or tablet into ¼ cup of cool water. Pour the rennet solution into the milk mixture and stir for 2 to 3 minutes. Cover the pot and allow the rennet to act upon the milk for 30 to 45 minutes, or until the curd breaks cleanly from the sides of the pot.

Cutting, draining and cooking the curd

Now that the curd is firm, cut into ½ cubes, making sure to cut all the way through to the bottom of the pot. Allow the cut curds to settle for 10 minutes.

Increase the heat and slowly raise the temperature of the curds to 124°F. Make sure that the temperature is raised slowly, no more than 2°F for every 5 minutes elapsed. Stir the curds often during this process.

Once the curds reach 124°F, continue stirring and hold the temperature there for an additional 20 minutes. The curds will shrink to the size of grains of rice. Test the curds at this point by squeezing a few grains between your fingers. They should be springy, almost rubbery. If the curds are still soft, continue cooking until they reach a rubbery texture, testing every 5 or 10 minutes.

Once ready, pour the curds into a cheesecloth-lined colander and allow to drain for 15 minutes.

Molding and Pressing the Curds

Spoon the drained curds into a cheesecloth-lined cheese mold. Pack the curds into the mold and fold the extra cheesecloth over the top of the curds.

Apply 5 pounds of pressure for 10 minutes. Flip the cheese over and apply the same 5 pounds of pressure for another 10 minutes.

Flip the cheese again and increase the pressure to 15 pounds for 1 hour. Flip once more and apply the same 15 pounds of pressure for an additional hour.

At this point, remove the cheese from the press and remove the cheesecloth. Line the mold with fresh cheesecloth and return the cheese, covering the top of the cheese with any extra cheesecloth. Apply 20 pounds of pressure to the cheese for 12 hours.

Once complete, remove the cheese from the mold and from the cheesecloth. Your cheese should be smooth and should not have any cracks. If you do find cracks, this means that your cheese has become too dry and was most likely over-cooked. Even with cracks, your cheese is fine, but remember to reduce your cooking time slightly when you make your next batch.

Brining and Aging

Prepare a brine solution by dissolving 2 cups of cheese, kosher or sea salt into 2 quarts of water in a stainless-steel bowl. Place the cheese into the solution and allow to float for 12 hours or overnight. Flip the cheese over and allow to float for an additional 12 hours.

Remove the cheese from the brine solution and set on a cheese mat, a rack or a plate. Place in your refrigerator and cover with a plastic bowl to retain the humidity, do not wrap at this point. Over time, your cheese will develop a natural rind that will protect the interior of the cheese. If you discover any mold, wipe the cheese with a fresh paper towel or fresh cheesecloth. After 2 months, rub your cheese with a thin coat of olive oil to help retain moisture. Your cheese will be ready to eat after about 3 months, but will have its best flavor after 6 to 10 months of continuous aging.

Swiss

Difficulty
Difficult

Time
3 hrs preparation
15 hrs pressing
4 weeks curing and drying
3-6 months aging

Storage
Several months when refrigerated

Weight
About 2 pounds

Milk
Cow's milk

Swiss cheeses, so named because they originated in the Alpine mountains are known for the holes found in the cheese and for its slightly sweet, nutty flavor. The holes in the cheese are caused by a bacterium, Proprionibacterium shermanii. The bacteria imparts the distinctive Swiss cheese flavor and produces carbon dioxide gas as a by-product, which causes the holes, or "eyes" as they are called. For the best flavor possible, age the cheese for 6 months.

Ingredients

> 2 gallons whole cow's milk
> ½ teaspoon liquid rennet, or ¼ crushed rennet tablet

1 ounce thermophilic starter , or ½ teaspoon thermophilic powder

1 teaspoon proprionic bacteria powder

Heating, Ripening & Renneting

Using your double boiler, slowly heat the milk to a temperature of 90°F. Lower the heat to maintain the 90°F temperature and stir in the thermophilic starter culture. Using a sterilized measuring cup, remove about ½ cup of the milk mixture and dissolve in the powdered proprionic bacteria. Stir to make sure that the powder dissolves and add the mixture back into your milk. Turn off the stove, cover the pot and allow to ripen for 20 minutes.

Dissolve the liquid rennet (or crushed rennet tablet) in ¼ cup of cool water in your sterilized measuring cup. Slowly pour the rennet mixture into the milk. Cover the pot again and allow the milk mixture to coagulate for 30 minutes. The curds should break cleanly from the sides of the pot. If more time is needed, check every 10 minutes until a clean break is achieved.

Cutting and Foreworking the Curds

Using your curd knife, cut the curd into ¼ inch cubes, making sure to cut all the way to the bottom of the pot. Use a ladle to slowly stir the curds to break them into smaller and smaller pieces.

For the next 40 to 45 minutes, maintain the curd temperature at 90°F while slowly stirring. Be patient, stirring too fast releases too much fat from the curds. At this stage, the curds will be about the size of grains of rice.

Cooking the Curds

Increase the heat on the curds to raise the temperature to 120°F. This must be done slowly, no more than 1°F per minute, for a total of about 30 minutes. Once the curds reach 120°F, lower the heat on your stove slightly so that you maintain a temperature of 120°F for another 30 minutes. Remember to keep stirring the curds often throughout this process.

To test the curds after cooking, use your ladle to remove a small sample of curds. Let them cool slightly so that you can handle easily. Make a small ball of curds in the palm of your hand. Rub the curds between your thumb and the palm of your hand. If the curds break apart easily, they are done. If they stick together, cook for another 10 to 15 minutes and test again.

Molding and Pressing the Curds

While the curds are still hot, ladle them into your sterilized cheese mold lined with cheesecloth. Be careful, as the whey that drains will be scalding hot, so place your mold in a basin or sink to avoid spilling.

Fold any extra cheesecloth over the top of the curds to completely cover them, insert a wood follower and apply 10 pounds of pressure for 30 minutes.

Remove the cheese from the mold. At this point, your cheesecloth will be soaked and small bits of curd will have squeezed through. Remove this cheesecloth and wrap your cheese in a fresh one. Return the cheese back into the mold and apply the same 10 pounds of pressure for another 30 minutes.

Remove the cheese from the mold and replace the cheesecloth again. Return to the mold and apply 15 pounds of pressure for 2 hours.

Remove the cheese from the mold, replace the cheesecloth once more and apply the same 15 pounds of pressure for 12 hours (overnight).

Brining, Curing and Aging the Cheese

Make a brine solution by dissolving 2 pounds of cheese, kosher or sea salt into 1 gallon of fresh, cool water. There will be a small amount of salt left on the bottom of your pot, which is an indication that no more salt can be dissolved into the water and your solution is thoroughly saturated. Remember, you must use a glass or stainless-steel bowl for this step. Using aluminum or any other material will produce unwanted flavors and ruin your cheese.

Prepare a dry, salted cloth by dipping a clean cheesecloth into the brine solution, wringing it out and hanging it to dry completely. Remove the cheesecloth from your cheese and float it into the brine solution. Set the whole pot into the refrigerator and allow the cheese to steep for 12 hours (overnight).

Remove the cheese from the brine solution and wipe dry with your salted cloth. Place on a clean cheese mat or cheese board and store in your refrigerator, making sure it is at or slightly above 50°F. Let the cheese set in the refrigerator for 1 week, turning twice per day. Once per day, wipe the cheese with your dry, salted cloth.

After 1 week of refrigeration, remove the cheese and allow to air-dry in a warm (70°F to 74°F) spot in your kitchen or pantry. Turn your cheese and wipe with your dry salted cloth once per day for 18 to 21 days. You will notice that the cheese will swell. While aging at this warmer temperature, the bacteria are forming the holes in the cheese that are so desired in Swiss cheese, causing it to swell.

For your last step to great Swiss cheese, transfer the cheese to you refrigerator or a room where the temperature and humidity can be controlled. For best results, store at 50°F, with high humidity (80% or greater). During this stage, the rind on the cheese will form and will show some discoloration. If any mold forms on the cheese, simply wipe away with your salted cloth. If the humidity is too low around your cheese, place a warm bowl of water next to it, and cover both under a large bowl, changing the water every few days. Allow your cheese to age for at least 3 months, and up to 6 months for the best flavor, if you can wait that long. Unfortunately, no one in my household has had the patience to wait that long!

Variations

Caraway Swiss

Not too long after making my first Swiss cheese, I sampled a store-bought Caraway Swiss cheese and had to try making my own version. The caraway seeds add a light, yet distinct flavor that I am sure you will enjoy. Prepare the seeds as you cook the Swiss cheese curds, as you will need to mix them into the curds after they are done cooking.

Preparing and Adding the Caraway Seeds

Boil one cup of water in a small saucepan. Add 3 tablespoons of caraway seeds and simmer for 10 minutes. Once you have finished cooking the Swiss cheese curds in the "Cooking the Curds" section, pour the seeds and water into the curds and stir thoroughly. Continue with the recipe as usual.

Mold And Bacteria Ripened Cheese

The most complex and time consuming of the cheeses, mold and bacterial ripened cheeses require extra time and care as either mold spores or extra bacterial cultures are added to the cheese which grow on or throughout the cheese during its aging process.

Follow the instructions in the book carefully. The addition of the extra bacteria or mold requires exacting procedures to make sure that your cheese develops perfectly.

"Cheese – milk's leap toward immortality."

Clifton Fadiman

"What happens to the hole when the cheese is gone?"

Berthold (The Adventures of Baron Munchausen)

American Brick

Difficulty
Moderate

Time
14 hrs plus aging

Storage
Up to two weeks
refrigerated

Weight
About 2 pounds

Milk
Cow's milk

Brick cheese was the first truly American cheese. It was developed in the United States late in the seventeenth century. Known for reddish colored bacteria that grows on the surface, it is creamy and very tangy, sharp flavor. I have heard the comparison that it is a cross between Cheddar and Limburger, but I assure you, the smell of the cheese is not that strong.

Ingredients
> 2 gallons whole cow's milk
> 2 ounces fresh mesophilic starter, or ½ teaspoon powdered

¾ teaspoon liquid rennet, or ¼ crushed rennet tablet

1 teaspoon bacterial linens powder

Cheese wax

Heating, Ripening & Renneting

Using your double boiler, heat the milk over low heat until it reaches a temperature of 85°F. Heat slowly, as this process should take 15 minutes. Add the starter culture to the milk, stirring thoroughly. Remove the mixture from the heat, cover and let stand to ripen for 20 minutes.

Dissolve the liquid rennet or the crushed rennet tablet into ¼ cup of cool water. Stir the solution into the milk mixture and stir thoroughly. Cover and let the mixture set for 45 minutes, or until the curd makes a clean break from the sides of the pot.

Cutting and Cooking the Curd

Once the curd has formed, use your curd knife to cut the curd into ½ inch cubes. Return the pot to the stove and slowly stir the curds to break them up with your ladle. Increase the heat to raise the temperature of the curds by 1°F every 5 minutes until they reach 92°F. This process should take at least 20 minutes.

Remove the pot from the heat and allow the curds to rest for 10 minutes.

Draining and Washing the Curds

During this step, you will need to drain some of the whey and replace it with warm, fresh water. This is the process of washing the curds. Fill a bowl with at least 5 or 6 cups of water at 92°F. Be sure to check the temperature of the water, as it must be at the same temperature as the curds (92°F).

Drain they whey down to the level of the curds. Add the warm, fresh water until it reaches the level that the whey was at before it was drained. Keeping the temperature at 92°F, stir the curds for the next 20 minutes. Remove from the stove and let the curds rest for 10 minutes.

Molding and Pressing the Curds

Ladle the curds into your 2-pound cheese mold that has been lined with cheesecloth. Cover the top of the curds with any extra cheesecloth and add your follower. Place 5 pounds of pressure on the cheese and press for 10 minutes. Remove the cheese and flip. Press again with 5 pounds for an additional 10 minutes.

Flip the cheese once more and press again with 5 pounds of pressure for 6 hours. Flip the cheese over once every hour.

Brining the Cheese

Remove the cheese from the press and remove the cheesecloth. Prepare a brine solution by dissolving 1 cup of salt into a glass or stainless steel bowl filled with ½ gallon of water.

Float the cheese into the brine solution and allow it to soak for 6 hours. Remove the cheese from the solution and set onto a cheese mat or rack to dry.

Adding Bacteria Linens

Sterilize a spray bottle and fill with 1 quart of cool water. Add the teaspoon of bacterial linens powder and shake until it is dissolved.

Spray your cheese with the bacteria solution. Be sure to cover all surfaces and soak your cheese thoroughly.

Return the cheese to the cheese mat and store it (uncovered) where the cheese can be kept at 60°F, with high humidity. Each day, gently wash the cheese with a salt-water solution (1/2 pound of salt to 1 gallon of water). Do not scrub the cheese, simply wet your hand with the salt-water solution and dampen all surfaces of the cheese.

After about 2 weeks, the cheese will have a reddish-brown color that is caused by the growth of the bacteria. At this point, rinse the cheese in cool water and dry with a paper towel.

Heat a block of cheese wax until it becomes liquid. Using a new or sterilized brush, cover the cheese completely with a layer of wax. Make sure that all surfaces of the cheese are covered and there are no cracks in the wax.

Let your freshly waxed cheese age in the refrigerator for 6 to 10 weeks before eating. Remember to turn the waxed cheese over a few times per week while it ages to prevent dry spots.

Camembert

Difficulty
   Hard

Time
   10 hrs plus aging

Storage
   Up to one week
   refrigerated

Weight
   About 2 pounds

Milk
   Goat's milk

Camembert is famous for its nutty, sooth taste. This cheese develops a natural white rind that can be eaten. Camembert cheese is not pressed, so it retains its smooth, almost flowing texture and is wonderful when heated.

For this recipe, you will need to use 4 Camembert cheese cylinders, cheese wrap and cheese mats. Camembert molds are available from cheese suppliers and allow the cheese to be drained properly. Along with these special molds, your will use large pans for draining, cheese mats and cheese boards.

Ingredients

> 2 gallons whole goat's milk
>
> ¼ teaspoon liquid rennet
>
> 4 ounces mesophilic starter culture, or 1 teaspoon powdered starter culture
>
> Penicillium candidum powder

Heating, Ripening & Renneting the Milk

Using your double boiler, warm the goat's milk slowly over a medium-low heat until it reaches a temperature of 90°F. Thoroughly blend in the mesophilic starter culture. Cover your pot, remove from the heat and allow to ripen for a total of 2 hours.

Dissolve ¼ teaspoon of liquid rennet in ¼ cup of cool water. Stirring slowly, blend in the rennet mixture. Cover your pot again and allow the milk mixture to work for 1 hour. At this time, the curds should break cleanly away from the sides of the pot. If not, cover again and allow the rennet to work longer and check every 10 minutes.

Cutting, Draining & Molding the Curds

Return your double boiler to the stove over low heat. Using your ladle, stir the curds to cut them as they warm. Stir the curds slowly, but continuously for 20 minutes while maintaining the temperature at

90°F. Then remove the pot from the heat and let rest for 20 minutes while you gather and sterilize your equipment for draining.

To drain the curds, you will need cheese mats, cheese boards, and large pans for the cheese to drain into. Place the cheese boards inside the pans, place a cheese mat on top of each board and place your molds on top of the mats.

Spoon the curds into the molds until full. On top of each of the filled molds, place another cheese mat and weigh down with either a plate or another cheese board.

Let the curds drain for 1 hour, then carefully flip each mold over without removing the cheese and let drain for an additional hour. Continue flipping and draining the curds until they have drained for a total of 6 hours. By this time, the curds will have shrunk to about 1 ½ inch high.

Molding & Aging the Curds

Remove the cheeses from the molds and sprinkle salt on all sides. In your sterilized spray bottle, dissolve a packet of the Penicillium candidium powder into 1 quart of cool water. Lightly spray all surfaces of each cheese.

Place the cheeses on a plate or cheese board and move to a refrigerator or basement where the temperature will remain at 40°F to 45°F and the humidity will remain near 90%.

Allow the cheeses to age and the mold to develop for 1 week. Once the white mold "fuzz" appears, flip the cheeses to allow the other side to grow evenly.

After a total of 14 days, wrap the cheeses in cheesewrap. Cheesewrap is available in specialty food stores and from cheese making suppliers. Cheesewrap is needed to ensure that the cheese can "breathe" properly while protecting it. You will definitely not get the same results using a regular cellophane wrap.

Store the wrapped cheese at 40°F to 45°F for 4 weeks, then enjoy!

Gorgonzola

Difficulty
Moderate

Time
2 days plus aging

Storage
Up to two weeks refrigerated

Weight
About 2 pounds

Milk
Cow or Goat

Named after a village near Milan, Italy, this cheese is similar to a standard blue cheese. It has a creamy and very rich flavor and a crumbly texture. Wonderful on salads, its sharp bite brings out the flavor of the vegetables. When making this cheese, you will ripen half of the milk one day and the other half the next day, so plan accordingly.

Ingredients

2 gallons whole cow or goat's milk

4 ounces mesophilic starter culture, or 1 teaspoon powdered starter culture

1 teaspoon liquid rennet, or ½ crushed rennet tablet

¼ teaspoon Blue mold powder (Penicillium roqueforti)
Cheese salt

Heating, Ripening & Renneting the Milk

Using your double boiler, warm just 1 gallon of milk over low heat until a temperature of 86°F is reached. Add 2 ounces of your mesophilic starter culture and stir thoroughly. Turn off the heat, cover and let the milk ripen for 30 minutes.

Dissolve ½ teaspoon liquid rennet (or ¼ crushed tablet) into ¼ cup of cool water. Stir the rennet solution into the milk, cover the pot and let the rennet work for 45 minutes. At this time, the curds should break cleanly from the sides of the pot. If not, allow additional time and check often.

Cutting & Draining the Curds

Using your long curd knife, cut the curd into ½ inch cubes and let rest for 10 to 15 minutes.

Line a colander with fresh cheesecloth and spoon in the curds to drain. Gather the corners of the cheesecloth and tie together. Hang the "bag" of curds over a pot and allow to drain at room temperature (70°F) overnight.

The next day, prepare a second batch of curds using the same method. Hand this "bag" of curds to drain for just 1 hour.

Unwrap the curds from the previous day and cut into 1-inch cubes and place in a glass or stainless steel bowl. Do the same with today's curds and place in a separate bowl.

In a small bowl, mix together 4 tablespoons of cheese salt and ¼ teaspoon of blue mold powder. Sprinkle half of this mixture into each bowl and gently stir in.

Molding the Cheese

Spoon about half of today's curds into the bottom and up the sides of the mold, making a cavity in the center. Place all of yesterday's curds into that cavity and top with the remaining curds you made today.

Place the mold on a board with a cheese mat. Place another cheese mat on to the top of the mold and cover with another cheese board or a plate. Topping the mold this way will make for easier turning.

For the next 2 hours, flip the mold over every 15 minutes.

Move the mold to a room, basement, or a section in your refrigerator where the temperature stays near 55°F and the humidity is maintained at 85%. Flip the cheese 2 or 3 times each day for 3 days.

Salting and Aging the Cheese

Remove your cheese from its mold and sprinkle all surfaces of the cheese with flake salt. Keep the cheese at the same 55°F temperature for 4 more days. Rub the cheese with flake salt once each day.

Using a sterilized ice pick or skewer, poke 25 to 30 holes in the cheese from the top all the way through the bottom. Return the cheese to age for 30 days. This produces air passages through the cheese that the bacteria will need to grow.

Move the cheese to a slightly cooler storage area where the temperature will remain at 50°F and the humidity will remain high at 85%. Allow the cheese to age for another 90 days. Every 2 or 3 weeks, scrape the mold and smear from the surface of the cheese with a knife.

Your cheese is now ready to eat. If you prefer a sharper cheese, it can be aged for several more months. After cutting, wrap tightly in cellophane and keep in the refrigerator.

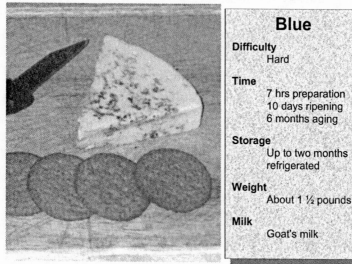

Blue

Difficulty
Hard

Time
7 hrs preparation
10 days ripening
6 months aging

Storage
Up to two months
refrigerated

Weight
About 1 ½ pounds

Milk
Goat's milk

All of the blue mold cheeses in this book require extra care and patience from the home cheese maker. The most difficult part is in the aging process where the temperature and humidity must be tightly controlled. The extra effort that is required in making this blue cheese recipe will be rewarded with a firm, creamy cheese you will be proud of. It is possible to use cow's milk with this recipe. Cow's milk will yield a cheese with a light yellow color and will taste quite well. If using cow's milk, increase the temperature in the first step from 86°F to 90°F.

Ingredients

2 gallons whole goat's milk

4 ounces mesophilic starter culture, or 1 teaspoon powdered culture

1 teaspoon liquid rennet, or ¼ crushed rennet tablet)

¼ teaspoon Blue Mold powder (Penicillium roqueforti)

Flake salt

Heating, Ripening and Renneting the Milk

Using your double boiler, slowly heat the milk over a medium-low stove until it reaches a temperature of 86°F. Thoroughly stir in the mesophilic starter culture, cover and let stand for 1 hour while maintaining the temperature at 86°F.

Dissolve the liquid rennet or crushed rennet tablet into ¼ cup of cool water. Add the rennet solution to the milk mixture and stir for 2 minutes. Cover and let the rennet work for at least 45 minutes, or until the curd makes a clean break from the sides of the pot, while maintaining a temperature of 86°F.

Cutting, Cooking and Draining the Curds

Using your long curd knife, cut the curd into ½ inch cubes. Once cut, let the curds rest for 10 minutes before stirring.

After letting the cut curds rest, gently stir with a ladle every 5 minutes for 1 hour. Maintain the same temperature of 86°F during this process.

Pour off as much whey as possible. Pour or ladle the curds into a stainless-steel colander that has been lined with fresh cheesecloth. Allow to drain for 10 minutes.

Return the curds to the pot and mix together with your hands to make sure that they are not sticking together.

Molding the Curds

Mix together 2 tablespoons of cheese salt and ¼ teaspoon of blue mold powder in a small bowl. Sprinkle the salt and mold mixture into the curds and gently mix together using your hands.

Place your cheese mold on top of a cheese mat and board. Fill the mold with the salted and molded curds. Cover the mold with another cheese mat and top with another cheese board or flat plate. Quite a lot of whey will be draining away, so place your mold where the whey can easily drain away.

Flip the mold over every 30 minutes for the next two hours. After the mold has been flipped for the last time, allow to rest overnight (12 hours).

Salting the Cheese

Remove the cheese from the mold and cover all surfaces with flake salt. Place the cheese on a cheese mat and move to a place where the temperature will remain at 60°F with humidity maintained at 85%.

Each day, for the next 3 days, flip the cheese and sprinkle with more flake salt.

Curing the Cheese

Using a sterilized ice pick or skewer, poke 25 to 30 holes from the top all the way through the bottom of the cheese. These holes will allow air to circulate through the cheese, helping the blue mold to form.

Store the cheese where the temperature will remain a constant 50°F, with humidity near 90%. A refrigerator will work well in keeping the temperature, but it is a good idea to place a bowl of warm water next to the cheese to help keep the humidity high, replacing it every other day.

Allow the cheese to cure for at least 10 days. Flip the cheese every 2 to 3 days while curing. At the end of this 10-day period, you should see blue mold beginning to cover the cheese.

Once the mold appears, allow it to grow for another 30 days or until the surface is covered. Gently scrape off the blue mold and slime from the surface of the cheese with a sterilized butter knife.

Allow to cure for another 90 days, scraping the cheese every 30 days.

After curing, scrape the cheese one last time and wrap tightly in plastic wrap or aluminum foil. Store the cheese in your refrigerator at 35°F to 38°F for another 3 months, turning weekly.

Your cheese will now be ready to sample. It will be smooth and creamy with a mild flavor. If you prefer a sharper, firmer cheese, allow to age for an additional 3 months. It is difficult to wait that long, but you will be rewarded.

Stilton

Difficulty
    Moderate

Time
    5 hrs preparation
    2 hrs molding
    3 days draining
    3 months aging

Storage
    Up to one month
    refrigerated

Weight
    1 ½ to 2 pounds

Milk
    Cow's milk

One of the most revered cheeses in Europe, Stilton hails from Nottinghamshire in England. Stilton has the soft, yet sharp flavor of Cheddar combined with the tangy taste of blue cheeses. As with most mold-ripened cheeses, it takes a long time to cure and age properly, but this Stilton recipe is one of the easiest of the blue cheeses to produce. This cheese pairs well with the sweetness of fruits, but is a wonderful snack all by itself on a cracker.

Ingredients
    2 gallons whole cow's milk
    2 ½ cups of heavy cream
    ½ teaspoons liquid rennet (or ¼ tablet)

2 ounces mesophilic starter culture (or ½ teaspoon powdered)

¼ teaspoon Blue mold powder

2 tablespoons cheese salt

Heating, Ripening & Renneting the Milk

In your double boiler, stir the heavy cream into the cow's milk. Warm the milk slowly over low heat until it reaches 86°F. Add your starter culture, cover and let ripen for 45 minutes while maintaining a temperature of 86°F.

Remove the cover and slowly stir in the liquid rennet until thoroughly mixed.

Continue top-stirring the mixture for several minutes. Top-stirring the milk mixture will prevent the cream from rising to the surface. Cover and let the milk set for 1 ½ to 2 hours while maintaining the temperature. At this point, the curd should make a clean break from the side of the pot. If not, let the mixture continue to set, checking every 10 minutes.

Cutting and Draining the Curd

Using your long curd knife, cut the curd into ½ inch cubes and allow to rest for 20 minutes.

Line a colander with cheesecloth. Place the colander into a sterilized bowl. Using your ladle, or a large slotted spoon, transfer the curds into the colander.

Let the curds rest in the colander, surrounded by the whey for 1 hour.

Tie the ends of the cheesecloth together in a knot and hang the "bag" of curds in a draft-free area for an additional 30 minutes, or until the curds stop dripping.

Move the bag of curds to a cheese board where it can drain and apply 5 pounds of pressure for at least 12 hours (overnight).

Milling and Salting the Curds

Remove the curds from the press and empty the solid curd into a sterilized bowl. Cut the curd into 1-inch cubes. In a separate bowl, blend together the 2 tablespoons of flake salt and ¼ teaspoon of Blue mold powder. Stir thoroughly. Sprinkle the mixture over the cut curds and blend together gently with your hands or a wooden spoon. Make sure that all of the curds are coated with the salt mixture.

Molding, Draining and Aging the Cheese

Place the curds into your cheese press, which is resting on top of a cheese mat and your cheese board. Cover the top of the mold with another cheese mat and top with another cheese board or plate. Allow the cheese to drain for 2 hours, flipping the cheese over every 30 minutes. Let the cheese continue to drain for the next 3 days, flipping several times each day.

Aging the Cheese

Remove your cheese from the mold and pierce it from top to bottom with a sterilized ice pick or skewer. Make at least 25 holes through the cheese. Place the cheese on a cheese mat and store in a cool room or refrigerator where the temperature will remain between 50°F and 55°F with humidity of at least 85%.

Once per week, gently scrape the mold and slime that grows on the surface with a sterilized butter knife. Allow the cheese to age for 4 months before tasting. If you prefer a sharper cheese and can wait that long, allow it to age for a total of 6 months.

Sources Of Cheesemaking Supplies

Please check out our website for supplies and advice about
making cheese and other foods such as sausages,
jams & jellies, breads, pickles and more!

Updates to this book, tricks, tips and techniques as well
as recipes are available 24 hours per day!

www.FoodHowTo.com

American Cheese Society

Website: www.cheesesociety.org
W 7702 County Road
Darien, WI 53114 (USA)

Newsletters, tips on cheese making,
member directories.

Caprine Supply

33001 West 83rd
Desoto, KS 66018 (USA)

Starter cultures, molds, kits, presses
and other supplies.

Cumberland General Store

Route 3, Box 81
Crossville, TN 38855 (USA)

Starter cultures and other cheese
making supplies.

Glengarry Cheesemaking

Website: www.cheese.com
RR #2
Alexandria, ON K0C 1A0
(Canada)

A large source for all cheese making
needs including equipment.

Lehman Hardware

Website: www.lehmans.com

P.O. Box 41
Kidron, OH 44636 (USA)

All sorts of cheese making supplies,
ingredients and equipment. One of
our favorite outside sources.

New England Cheesemaking

Instructional workshops, education

Website: www.cheesemaking.com and cheese making supplies.

85 Main Street
Ashfield, MA 01330

About The Author

Shane Sokol is one of the few natives of Florida that still lives there. He lives on the west-coast of Florida with his wife, Marie, and their "too many" cats. An avid food-lover, he has been making his own cheeses for years. Other food related hobbies include beer and wine making, bread making, canning and preserving. Shane and Marie hope you've enjoyed this book. Several other books about food are planned. Please surf on over to Shane and Marie's website for more information about upcoming books, recipes and tips. Their website is located at: *http://www.FoodHowTo.com*

Bibliography

Brown, Bob. The Complete Book of Cheese. New York: Gramercy, 1960

Carroll, Ricki and Carroll, Robert. Cheesemaking Made Easy. Vermont: Storey Books, 1996

Ciletti, Barbara J. Making Great Cheese. North Carolina: Lark Books, 1999

Edelman, Edward. The Ideal Cheese Book. New York: Harper & Row, 1986

Eekhof-Stork, Nancy. The World Atlas of Cheese. New York: Paddington Press, 1976

Harbutt, Juliet. Cheese. Wisconsin: Willow Creek Press, 1999

Jenkins, Steve. Cheese Primer. New York: Workman, 1996

Jones, Evan. The World of Cheese. New York: Knopf, 1976

Meyer, Carolyn. Milk, Butter, and Cheese: the Story of Dairy Products. New York: Morrow, 1974

Nanet, Bernard. Cheeses of the World. New York: Rizzoli, 1993

Pearl, Anita-May. Completely Cheese. New York: Jonathan David Publishers, 1978

Radke, Don. Cheese Making at Home: the Complete Illustrated Guide. New York: Doubleday 1974

Index